Dear Julianne,

May the goddess always

continue to bless you on

your path of heart.

Deep love,

18·09·24

Shamanism
as Medicine

An initiation into the world of Shamanism

C L A U D I A   G O N C A L V E S

BALBOA.PRESS
A DIVISION OF HAY HOUSE

Balboa Press books may be ordered through booksellers or by contacting:

Balboa Press
A Division of Hay House
1663 Liberty Drive
Bloomington, IN 47403
www.balboapress.co.uk
UK TFN: 0800 0148647 (Toll Free inside the UK)
UK Local: (02) 0369 56325 (+44 20 3695 6325 from outside the UK)

Print information available on the last page.

ISBN: 978-1-9822-8486-2 (sc)
ISBN: 978-1-9822-8488-6 (hc)
ISBN: 978-1-9822-8487-9 (e)

Balboa Press rev. date: 10/19/2022

To my children now, and to my grandchildren and great-grandchildren to come:

I leave to you this legacy, the legacy of my life and my love for you and humanity, which I discovered I had when I looked deep beneath my pain.

This book is my offering to the loving spirits who
work with me as a continuation of their work.
I am ready to let go!

Contents

Acknowledgements.. ix

Introduction... xi

Chapter 1   The Shaman-Healer....................................... 1

Chapter 2   Moon Cycle and the Spirits............................ 29

Chapter 3   Misappropriation, Misconception, Misunderstanding..... 59

Chapter 4   Shamanism and Self-Care 74

Chapter 5   The Return of the Divine Feminine................... 92

Chapter 6   Talking to Spirits—My Personal Quest to Learn
             about Healing... 106

Chapter 7   Well-Being and Healing................................. 120

Chapter 8   My Experience of the Vision Quest.................... 128

Afterword... 165

About the Author.. 167

Acknowledgements

I would like to thank everyone who made the publication of this book possible. I am eternally grateful to

- My teachers and loving spirits who bring so much light and joy to my life.
- My loving, caring, and supportive husband Mark Halliday: I love you!
- My children, who are now young adults, Thomas and Gloria, for their patience, love, and everyday teachings. They both carry the names of two very important centenary elders as their middle names: Elviro and Alice. I believe this is the reason why they have always been ahead of their time. You are the bright stars of my life.
- All the people who, by trusting me as their shamanic teacher, have provided me with the opportunity to learn, open up, trust, love, be of service, and be compassionate.
- My parents and grandparents: With your ways, I have learnt to balance unconditional love, service, and compassion with ruthless compassion.
- All the people who have volunteered and still volunteer at the Planetary Healing Centre and the Edinburgh Shamanic Centre: we share the same vision of a compassionate world, a world without suffering. You became my spiritual family. You are the proof that the burning fire of love and the ability to serve another human being is a capacity that all human beings have, without exception.

- My first editor, Fiona Scott Patrick, for her superb skills and deep encouragement.
- The elders and teachers around me: Watsu Yawanawa (Leticia), Sr Antonio Apuriná, Pajé Sr Santo Kulina (Maná), Radsuha Kulina, Pajé Sheterru Shanenawa, Pajé Waxy Yawanawa, Susan Stanton, Stewart Keith, Alma Shearer, Emily Boyd, Margaret Harper, Sue Tait, Margot Daru-Elliot, Tessa McKirdy, Anne Fowler, Dorothy Forester: thank you for your service to humanity, your support, your time, your wisdom, your teachings, and your friendship.
- The elders and teachers who are now in the spirit world: Dona Mercedes, Elviro Chino, Tata Txanu Natasheni (Tata Yawanawa), Ann Henderson, and Jed Pemberton.

Introduction

It is my intention that *Shamanism as Medicine* helps you on your journey and helps to focus your light. We might know who we are, where we come from, and of the love we carry in our hearts, but if we are not able to focus our light—the energy and light that we have and carry—then it can easily disperse.

My spiritual journey began at a very early age, when I was immersed in darkness, fear, and despair. It was but a few years later when I was to catch a glimpse of my light, and it was at that point that I began to understand why I came into being; it was only then that I understood my soul's purpose in this lifetime.

However, the journey has not always been sweetness and light, as I have strayed from the path—many times. I have forgotten who I am, and I have walked in and out of darkness time after time.

One of my early teachers was my grandmother Honorata. She was a *benzedeira*, a medicine woman, and she taught me unconditional love. The love she carried for others poured out from her so abundantly that I was lucky enough to drink from it many times in my early childhood and teenage years. She passed into the spirit world when I was only seventeen years old. It took another seventeen years for me to begin to understand that our connection was only just beginning. And when I opened up to the spirit world, she would go on to be the most present person in my life, continuing to nurture my spirit, my mind, my heart, and my soul. It was from the spirit world that her presence in my life was truly felt. She would come into my dreams to teach me and heal me. It was never clear to me if it was her calling me or me calling her when those dreams occurred. She is always present when I do the sacred transmissions in the Feather Stone Energy Healing work. She is my loving grandmother, in my blood I carry unconditional love passed down to me from her. It was from her that I started to learn the ways of compassion.

My maternal grandfather Joaquín Pereira was also my teacher. He taught me about humility, generosity, and patience—the balanced side of the masculine is patience. He pulled me out of the river when I nearly drowned at age five, so I owe him my life—twice! I therefore offer back to him the gift of my life filled with unconditional love.

I was truly fortunate to learn ruthless compassion from my other grandmother, Vicentina. Her mother was purely indigenous. Indigenous gifts are passed down from the ancestors to the younger generations by blood and/or memory. From her I learnt the indigenous ways of walking my talk. Her legacy to me was *truth*, the truth that hardly anyone has the courage to speak, the truth that shakes us to our core. From her I learnt the ways of the warrior: truth and impeccability with self and others. It has taken me half a century to make peace with my grandmother Vicentina and, in turn, to make peace with myself.

Another teacher was elder Dona Mercedes. She came into my life when I was nine years old. When I was thirteen, she decided I needed to be initiated in the ways of the healer. She taught me to take my first steps of the conscious walk that is the spiritual path of the healer. When we are blind or in darkness, we need help to see. We need someone to guide our steps, someone we can trust. Dona Mercedes was that guide for me. She stepped into my life and stayed present like a rock throughout my teenage years. To this day, now from the spirit world, she continues to show me the way: every time I do energy healing work, she guides my hands.

Another teacher came later, this one in my early twenties. His name was Elviro, lovingly called *Chino* by those who met him and loved him.

His simplicity and his healing and loving ways touched so many. He was supposedly one hundred and four years old when he passed into the spirit world, but he always argued he was much older because he had only been registered after his adopted father took him from the shores of the Amazon river when Elviro was aged three or five. His adopted father was a white man who believed he was saving an indigenous child lost in the Amazon jungle. However, Elviro does not recall being lost; instead, he recalls playing by the riverside. Whatever the case may be, the Great Spirit clearly had plans for Elviro as he became a great shaman, teacher, and healer for anyone who sought his teachings. He lived in a little house at the top of a mountain in Leme, right beside Copacabana beach, one of the most famous places in Rio de Janeiro. Elviro taught me that I *was* loved. He taught me that I could trust myself and have confidence in *me*, in who *I am*. So I began to remember who *I* am and where *I* come from, and therefore I now know where *I* am going. My son bears Elviro's name as his father and I wanted to honour Elviro and the light that he brought into our early adult lives. He showed me the ways of my indigenous ancestors.

Then in my late forties I met another indigenous teacher who was also one hundred and four years old, Tata Yawanawa. I participated in the last Ayahuasca ceremony facilitated by Tata. When he passed to the spirit world a month and a half later, I felt the expansion of his spirit in many directions. It was as if his spirit had entered thousands of the people who loved him. His spirit came to me and told me to go to Brazil to learn from the indigenous people and also to help them, as they needed help. So it was that in 2016 I began the Indigenous Peoples Project and a bridge of light began to form between Scotland and Brazil.

I have had many other teachers, too many to mention here. Some of them are still in my life today. I honour and treasure them all.

When I was thirty-three years old, the same age as my great-grandmother when she passed to the spirit world, something really important happened: I entered the sacred womb of the mother, and in that sacred sweat lodge I had a rebirth. After that rebirth, the spirits became my teachers and taught me the ways of the shaman-healer. Reality and the world have never been the same again.

It is my hope that *Shamanism as Medicine* will help you to focus your light. I have dreamt about this book for over twenty years. Only when I had fully learnt how to focus my light was I able to write about it and share with you in book form.

May your journey be blessed and your path illuminated by the light you have within you. When we walk the shaman-healer's path, we walk on our own, yet we are never alone, for our path is filled with Great Spirit.

> —Called Cláudia Gonçalves by my parents, Standing Stone by the spirits, Tyvan (Warrior Woman) by the Yawanawa and Xanupa by the Apuriná people

CHAPTER 1

The Shaman-Healer

A shaman-healer is a man or a woman who serves his or her community and seeks the spiritual well-being of the people within that community. Shaman-healers seek higher knowledge from Spirit and use it to serve their people, using their newfound knowledge to maintain the balance between the people and the spirits of all things.

While almost anyone can train to become a shaman-healer and develop his or her shamanic skills, it is ultimately the spirits who choose who will be taken farther along the path to apprentice directly with the spirits. Accessing states of higher consciousness involves awareness of interwoven realities. In these interwoven realities, or webs of light, the shaman-healer travels spiritually to do his or her work as healer, diviner, soul retriever, bridge, messenger, or guide for lost souls.

Becoming a shaman-healer involves establishing a relationship with the powers of Creation. There are infinite numbers of ways to do this: prayers, fasting, medicine walks, shamanic journeys, meditation, initiations, sacred ceremonies, vision quests, death lodges, sacred peace pipe ceremonies, earth lodges, rites of passage, sweat lodges, and sacred plant medicines, amongst other things. Ceremonies offer ways for us to establish a connection and communication with the out-of-the-ordinary reality or world of spirit.

Traditions and the ways in which shamanism is expressed vary depending on one's culture, but the essence is the same: shamanism is about establishing a connection with the spirit world to bring healing and insights to the physical world for members of the community.

Shaman-healers start with the connection to spirit, the connection with the spirit guides. This involves entering into what we call a *shamanic state of consciousness* in order to receive or access information given to us from the spirit world through the spirit guides.

When a shaman-healer is connecting with spirit, he or she has to be seen and respected by the spirits in the spirit world. This respect is predicated on the healer's clear intent, integrity, and purity of heart. It is only after they observe these attributes that the spirits become allies, serving the shaman-healer and assisting with his or her work. The initiation into the spirit world then begins. Humility and purity of heart are important on the shamanic path: without humility and purity of heart, the highest spirits cannot see the shaman-healer's light. The more the shaman-healer develops his or her consciousness, the more help he or she will receive from the highest spirits.

The initiation into the spirit world can be testy and vigorous, and being faced with so many difficulties on the path ahead can sometimes make shaman-healers apprehensive. The challenges are there, though, as a way of learning and self-development in order to support and empower the shaman-healer on his or her path of service.

It is true that, as people of many vocations do, healers start their shamanic journeys by experiencing a definite calling. Not all hear the call enter this world, and out of the ones who do, just a few answer. This is largely down to the most basic human condition, fear—humans' earliest and most profound emotion. Other times, the sheer arduousness of the path can discourage the shaman-healer's calling.

Validation for the healer's work comes largely from the members of the community who sought the help from the healer in the first place. After the shaman-healer's initiation from spirit to community and community to spirit, his or her lifelong relationship with the spirits begins.

Shamanism is the earliest-known spiritual path in human history; it has been studied and practised by all the earth's original societies. The fundamentals of shamanism are a testimony of the truth: that *all* is interconnected and everything has a spiritual nature to it.

While other spiritual and religious practices merely require practitioners to adhere to a specific set of rules, shamanism is, in every way, a way of living. The basics of shamanism involve acknowledging and interacting with the world of spirit, which in turn reconnects us to our Earth Mother.

It is fair to say that on the shamanic path there are no masters. There is no room for ego. All there is, is mastery of the self.

Alignment of Heart, Mind, and Spirit

Often people walk around completely misaligned: their heart wants one thing, but their actions end up doing something different because their hearts, minds, and spirits are not aligned. This can cause a lot of internal conflict and wrong decisions—bad decisions that will affect a person's life for a long time, not to mention the diseases this misalignment can bring. So the spirits have taught me, and tell me, to teach others how to align heart, mind, and spirit.

In a shamanic healing session for men, you, the shaman-healer, align the heart to the mind and the mind to the spirit. In a session for women, you align the womb to the heart, the heart to the mind, and the mind to the spirit.

Before the alignment, you need to clear each energy centre in the respective areas of the body. After the cleansing is done, you create a bridge of light between the person's heart and mind. You bring your hands to the person's heart and see, feel, and visualise a bridge of light coming out of his or her heart and into his or her mind. I say *feel* because for you to

3

effect change in any reality, you need to bring all aspects of yourself, mind, heart, and spirit, together. The mind thinks it, the heart feels it, and the spirit visualises it. If you visualise that bridge of light at least three times, it will be there.

The number three is significant in that it carries a code, an energy, and a power, namely the power of the three aspects of the divine: maiden, mother, and crone. Alternatively, you might say mother, father, and child, depending on what tradition you come from.

When you are creating that bridge between the heart and the mind, you are changing the person's energy. You are affecting the person's life on a very deep level, as no longer will he or she walk confused, and no longer will he or she make wrong decisions—decisions based only in the mind, for example. A new dimension will begin to emerge in the person's life. His or her heart will become stronger, enhanced by his or her feelings, and he or she will begin to have more clarity and understanding of all aspects—and consequences—of his or her decisions. The person begins to make his or her decisions based on whether a choice sounds good, feels good, and is good.

A person who walks with his or her heart and mind aligned can feel the beauty of life, can better appreciate, and begin to be in better harmony with, what is around him or her. Why? Simply because the person has begun to live from the heart and no longer says one thing and does another. The person will always say what is in his or her heart. That alone will unblock the energy pathways in the body. More light will come in, and there will be more space. Even the cells in the person's body will feel aligned with truth on a cellular level.

After the alignment of heart and mind, the person will benefit from the alignment of the mind and the spirit, as they are interconnected. We can align both the heart and the mind, and the mind and the spirit, by visualising a bridge of light. Visualise and feel a bridge of light between the mind and the spirit just above the crown chakra, which sits a few centimetres above the top of the head.

By aligning the spirit to the mind, you change the way the person lives life and thereby enable him or her to live a more fulfilled life aligned with his or her spiritual purpose—the reason the individual came to this earthly realm in the first place. We all came here to do more than just make money, have the best car, gain a high position in a company, or purchase a nice house or a boat. Yes, we came here to do those material things, but we also came here to do much greater things, things that go beyond the physical and material plane.

That something that we are meant to do is blocked; our energy systems become clogged; our minds have forgotten; and for a long time we just wander around distracted, without truly remembering why we came to this beautiful planet called Earth. However, you see, when our minds and spirits become aligned, all of that begins to change. A sense of purpose begins to emerge, an understanding that there is something really important we came here to do. And what is more, that purpose begins to appear. We then begin to remember, as the bridge between the mind and the spirit has now been repaired and reconnected. The shaman-healer, with his or her understanding and ability to move energies, puts his or her hand in the mind centre and in the spirit centre and then repairs the bridge. The bridge is broken at birth. The birthing in this earthly realm is one of the traumatic experiences we endure as human beings.

All aspects of reality can be changed or altered by shaman-healers, who have themselves done a significant amount of healing and repairing of themselves. A shaman-healer understands that all is energy and that energy is movable, changeable, especially when one starts to focus with heart intention, bringing feelings to it. Scientists are only just beginning to understand the vibrations of the heart field and how this powerhouse centre works.

By combining the powerhouse of the heart, the powerhouse of the mind, and the powerhouse of the spirit, we humans become unstoppable. We become super powerhouses, manifesting our thoughts, the material things we need, and help comes our way from others. We gain the ability to create projects, dreams, and visions, be it for oneself or for others. On the shamanic path we call this ability *spiritual power*.

Now, it is not spiritual power the way in which most people think. It is a spiritual power in the sense of remembering who we are, connecting with our blueprint, remembering why we came to this earthly realm at this time, and discovering how we can bring harmony to all around us through our thoughts, feelings, and actions in the world. It might sound complex, but it is not. It is actually very simple: by living in alignment with the truth in our hearts, living a life in alignment with our higher spiritual purpose, our every action, every thought, and every feeling is full to the brim with the highest intention, the highest energy, and the highest love.

One might think, *This is all very well, but that is not possible!* Other thoughts might include, *I have outbursts of anger, rage, violence, and people really get on my nerves!* or *My heart wants one thing, and life gets in the way and I do something else.*

Well, perhaps try to see it this way: everything is possible. That moment of anger, rage, or violence is gone; it does not exist in this moment. All that there is, is this moment. What are you doing for this moment that you have, to become a moment of peace, truth, and alignment with your highest purpose, your higher self? This is what really matters. What you are doing now, not what you have done a minute ago, or what you will be doing in the future—none of that exists. You are left with the now, so what are you doing with the now that you have? That is what is important.

When a person is brought into alignment, it becomes clear that his or her energy has started to change. It might change gradually, slowly, but it changes. Everything is very subtle. One needs to be highly tuned in to oneself to be able to notice the subtle yet powerful changes that take place. The path then begins to open; the energy is unblocked. Deep and profound changes begin to unfold.

After the alignment, the person's soul is then brought down fully into the body with intent and love. It is now safe to be in the body. It is now safe to live from the heart, in alignment with a spiritual purpose.

Ayahuasca as a Healing Medicine

> The land of healing lies within, radiant with the happiness
> that is blindly sought in a thousand other directions.
> —Swami Vivekananda

A long time ago, a shaman or a medicine person only practised shamanism in a tribal context and dedicated his or her life to it. Most of the teachings were somehow kept secret and passed down orally to the next in line or to the next young person learning the art.

At the beginning of the twentieth century, however, a change in the human psyche meant that people sought out shamans and medicine people for their teachings and that people became eager to learn their practices. Today, more and more people are seeking to learn the art of shamanic healing, and shamanic teachings, to incorporate it into their everyday lives for health and well-being. Think the yoga revival, the radical departure in yoga from the East to the West. Shamanism also began the long journey from the jungles of the world into the homes of the cities, reaching wherever the people were.

With the blossoming of shamanism around the world and more and more contact with native indigenous ways, interest in Ayahuasca has also boomed around the world. There is no mistaking that Ayahuasca healing has made a big impact on Westerners. Millions make the trip to places such as Peru, the most popular destination. Others travel to Brazil or Central America for the medicine, whether this may be to discover one's life purpose, find deeper meaning, or heal old wounds. Whatever the reason, it is clear that the numbers travelling to encounter the sacred medicine are still growing.

The First Ayahuasca World Conference took place in Ibiza in October 2014, organised by the International Center for Ethnobotanical Education, Research, and Service (ICEERS). More than six hundred people from all over the world were at that conference.

The Second Ayahuasca World Conference took place in my homeland, Brazil, in the state of Acre in the Amazon in October 2016, with a turnout of nearly one thousand people from all over the world including hundreds of indigenous people.

The Third Ayahuasca World Conference took place in Girona in Spain at the end of May 2019, this time with a turnout of more than one thousand and five hundred people. The numbers keep growing.

In Brazil, the journey of Ayahuasca towards humanity began at the "Boca to Acre", where the river Acre, also called the Amazon river, begins the journey to meet the waters of the world. Even though the 2016 conference was in a remote part of Brazil with very few flights going there, people came from all four corners of the world, by land, by sea, and by air. The indigenous people were represented and very present contributing to the conference. It was time to hear what the indigenous people had to say about the use of the sacred medicine of Ayahuasca by others.

One may ask the question: Why the sudden interest in a medicine used by the indigenous people for millennia? It is my humble belief that is because this sacred medicine could hold the key for the next revolution that humanity will experience in consciousness, which will be coupled with a revolution in health and well-being in all its aspects: mental, physical, emotional, and spiritual health. Humanity is at the edge of *something*, and we are not being able to cope with what our modern life has thrown our way. It feels as if we have made a mess out of our existence and we need something really big and strong to bring us back to our senses. Ayahuasca is that medicine, a medicine that can potentially save humanity from a catastrophic ending.

However, sacred medicines must be approached with the utmost respect and deep care. Ayahuasca should not be viewed as some kind of magic potion. Lovingly called by some as the Sacred Mother, Ayahuasca is the mixing of two plants, one masculine and one feminine. We have to remember that when the powers of the masculine forces and the powers of the feminine forces come together, new consciousness is born—life is created. Thus, Ayahuasca has the power to create a *new consciousness* in humankind on the earth, a consciousness that is more compassionate, less traumatic, less painful, less attached, and less earthbound. The Sacred Medicine is also known as the "Vine of Death" because she can bring death to our ego, end our attachments, heal our traumas, and heal our diseases.

Ayahuasca has the power to give life to one again and to heal and transform when taken the right way. Equally, it has the power to cause and exacerbate mental diseases if taken the wrong way. When the latter is the case, one can also get *stuck* or *lost* in the spirit world, unable to find his or her way back here. The experience sometimes can be a bit overwhelming, like opening Pandora's box and getting, well, more than one bargained for. Vitally important, and this rule cannot be stressed enough, one must approach Ayahuasca with the right awareness and with the respect the medicine deserves. Like every powerful medicine, it can cause many problems if taken incorrectly, so it must not be taken under the counter or be given by an unqualified "doctor". Therefore, I recommend caution for anyone who feels the call or need for this powerful medicine.

Sometimes shaman-healers drink the medicine to diagnose people who come to them for healing. In some cases, the "patient" may not drink the medicine for a long time, or until the shaman-healer knows when the patient is ready to take it.

For a long time, I held in my heart that we do not need the aid of anything, only the aid of the spirits, to accomplish the work, so I did not feel I needed to work with the sacred medicine. However, over the years I began to understand more about the need for spiritual medicine in our modern world. In 2003 I began my journey back home to my homeland of Brazil to meet and work with the spirit of Ayahuasca as my teacher.

Ayahuasca is a spirit herself, so I asked my helping spirits why humanity was making such a fuss about the sacred medicine. The spirits lovingly explained that sometimes traumas that we might take up to ten years to clear with psychotherapy, counselling, medication, and so forth, are able to clear up very quickly with the spirit of Ayahuasca working in conjunction with a shaman-healer and other spirit helpers.

Sometimes, depending on the power of the shaman-healer and the spirits he or she works with and how long the person has been suffering, it may take quite a few Ayahuasca ceremonies for *dis-eases* to begin to be lifted.

The spirits also told me that it is not just drinking the medicine that matters. A shaman-healer who knows how to work with energies, with spirits, and with the aid of the Ayahuasca spirit can transmute and transform the trauma and uproot it very quickly. Taking the medicine on your own or with a group of people, or with just *any* facilitator, will not do the trick.

In some ways, drinking Ayahuasca without a shaman-healer is like having an operation performed on you by a nurse or by yourself, when what you need is a highly experienced surgeon.

So it is that for me, drinking Ayahuasca when I have deep trauma is akin to going in for surgery. If the person facilitating the delivery of the medicine is not an experienced shaman-healer, then one runs the risk of being sliced open on the operation table, only to walk out with one's guts or one's brain, one's energy body, completely exposed.

For those who feel the call to work with this powerful medicine, I recommend contact with the indigenous people, to drink and to learn from them. An apprenticeship can take a minimum of twelve years and a maximum of a lifetime.

For those who feel the call to drink the sacred medicine for healing, I would say not to rush into the matter. I recommend caution when you hear of people facilitating ceremonies. Ask, where did they learn? Whom did they apprentice with? For how long did they apprentice and develop their relationship with the medicine? What is their shamanic background, and how much do they know about working with energies, spirits, plant spirits, entities, and healing? Are they in it just for themselves, for power, ego, or money, or are they in it because they genuinely want to heal and help others? All these are important questions you need to ask if you are considering taking part in an Ayahuasca ceremony, even if it is one that you have heard loads about or one that your best friend invited you to.

There is another aspect to consider: since Ayahuasca has many contraindications such as heart problems, liver problems, mental health problems, breathing problems, and problematic interactions with certain medications, the facilitator must have considerable knowledge of the effects of taking the medicine and the contraindications, including the various aspects and levels. So a screening process is really important to safeguard participants.

Look for someone who has apprenticed with indigenous people and is experienced with all aspects of the medicine used in modern context. Such people should also have equal experience working shamanically with spirits, energy, and entities. Look for someone who works with the plant in a sacred and ceremonial way. If you cannot find such an individual near you, then a few journeys to Central or South America might be the right investment for your health and well-being.

Ayahuasca medicine is illegal around the world, even in countries such as Brazil and Peru, which hold the medicine as a spiritual cultural heritage. Brazil is currently undergoing more than a ten-year running process, involving the government, all Santo Daime churches, and most recently the indigenous people, to decide if the medicine should be legal or not in Brazil. Yet in 2021, with the issue of legality still being undecided, in Brazil there is some leniency with regard to people using the sacred medicine. Unlike in some other countries, you do not go to jail in Brazil for running ceremonies. But the Brazilian authorities will confiscate the medicine if one is caught with it.

A shaman once told me that the fact that Ayahuasca medicine is illegal around the world is a good thing. It protects the sacred medicine. In many ways, it brings a form of respect to the medicine. We have to remember that legalising the medicine is not going to help protect the medicine.

The sacred medicine should not fall into the hands of "children" who do not understand the power of the two plants that come together in the sacred union to create consciousness and open the doorways to other dimensions.

Sometimes traumas and other dimensions are better left alone if one is not ready to understand, or is not strong enough to cope with what one sees or learns, or if one does not have someone strong enough and with the right skills and experience to help one deal with the issue at hand.

Most indigenous people are not against the use of the medicine by the people of the world, but they do feel strongly that people need to seek their counsel and learn from them first before starting offering ceremonies. They need to learn the tradition and the correct way to use the medicine.

If you ask me whether Ayahuasca should, or should not, be used outside the context of the jungle, my reply is this: I have deep respect for radical warriors who are revolutionaries, but I am not a radical warrior myself, as it goes against my nature as a healer. As a person born as a Libra, holding the symbol of justice, I always look for the truth on both sides. I also see what each side loses when one side wins. Not everything is black or white, and sometimes we can choose the grey area in between, where we can live happily. One thing is true on this matter or any matter: *discernment is paramount.* Choosing the most experienced surgeon to operate on you might come to your benefit in the end.

What to Look for in a Teacher

There is no university degree or accreditation required to become a shaman-healer.

It is my view that everyone is born with a shamanic gift, which is simply the ability to interact with the spirit world and help others. It's a little bit like art; everyone is born with the ability to draw, scribble, and move the paintbrush left and right. Anyone who takes considerable time and is dedicated to learning and practising has the potential to become an artist. So the answer lies in developing one's own gift by learning as much as possible of the shamanic art and applying it as much as possible to one's life, helping oneself with the ailments of the mind, body, and spirit and helping others when one is ready to do so. Practice and dedication leads to perfection.

When we begin to study and practice the art of shamanism, we are all taking responsibility for ourselves and are empowered when it comes to our own health and well-being.

What should you look for when seeking a shamanic teacher? First, check where the person has started to learn the art himself or herself. I say *started* because in shamanism it is not possible to say that one has learnt it all, or become a master, or has a degree, for in shamanism, no matter if you are practising for a year, ten years, fifty years, or even eighty years, you, like everyone, are at the beginning. There is no end to the beginning, and there is always a new beginning to the end.

For the shaman, life is a learning playground. On the shamanic path, the more one learns, the more there is to learn. Shamans learn from every person he or she encounter, no matter how short the encounter, as it is an encounter in a lifetime. On this path, everyone is a teacher and everyone is a student.

If you encounter a shamanic practitioner or a teacher who makes you feel that he or she is above you in any respect, know that this person has nothing to teach you which will truly enhance your life.

A good shamanic teacher holds true humbleness in his or her heart, in his or her aura, in his or her *being* in the world. Such an individual is not presumptuous or scary in any way and is not forceful or in-your-face. The best teacher is the one who goes about his or her own business. Often such teachers are so busy supporting and healing people in their community that they have no time for clamouring or putting themselves out there as a *show* business. Those still in that stage of their lives have not yet moved to the place of adulthood and true community and service. They are still in the place of the teenager who needs to be seen to feel better inside. Such people need a lot of healing themselves.

Look for a teacher who has done a considerable amount of work on himself or herself, someone who has no need for the limelight.

How does training come into shamanism? Can a person really train in shamanism and then become a shamanic healer? In shamanism, we do not give ourselves the title of "shaman"; the title comes from the community—if they are happy with you as their healer. If they feel you really help them heal their ailments, their anxieties, and their imbalance of mind, body, and spirit, then they call you a shaman-healer and begin sending their friends to see you because you have helped them and because they know that you will help their friends too. They trust you because you have consistently shown that you truly work to be of service to another.

How many times have you had to get out of your bed to serve another, when all you wanted was to stay in your own comfortable bed? How many times have you done this when someone else needed your help, because someone else was suicidal, because someone else was suffering, or because someone else had to have an entity that was "doing his or her head in" removed from his or her energy field? Your bed is nice and comfortable, and you can get back to it later, but in that moment you have to go because the spirits you work for have called for you. And in shamanism, there is no space for laziness or leaving it for later, doing half a job, or paying someone else to do your job.

A good shamanic teacher is not just someone who has years of training and holds a title; a good teacher is someone who truly walks the talk and lives his or her life by what he or she preaches. You will enrich your life by observing and learning from that kind of teacher more than you would by sitting and having papers and books filled with talk and no walk thrown at you.

In shamanism, you also learn by doing—by having a community you support, by creating a project that the community truly needs, and by dedicating your life to and doing it without expecting anything in return. That is what true service is, and when you truly serve, it gives you experience and true access to the spirit world.

A good way to gain experience in service is to volunteer. The time when I learnt the most was when I volunteered as a shamanic healer one day a week for seven years in our holistic health project at the Community Foundation for Planetary Healing, a charity my husband and I cofounded in Edinburgh. If there are no opportunities for volunteering near you, then create your own project: volunteer your medicine once a week or once a month to those in real need who cannot afford to pay for a full session with you. You can also volunteer to work for children. Children need help too, and parents may not always have enough money for sessions for their children. So offering one or two shamanic sessions for free or donating one day a week or one day a month is a good way to learn about true service.

When I was volunteering, I was seeing three people a day every time I was in the project. Those years of volunteering gave me the real experience I needed, and it was through that experience that the inspiration for creating all the training courses offered at the Edinburgh Shamanic Centre came into being. I learnt so much about people, diseases, entities, and attachments, as well as about people's empowerment through shamanism.

No other place, no other training school, and no number of years of contact with indigenous people in a tribal context could have ever given me what I was gifted through those years of volunteering. More than anything, I learnt to serve—to serve without expecting payment, to serve without doing it for the money I would receive at the end, to serve just for the pure joy that serving brings to the heart.

Thinking back, I realise that was the best training I've ever received. The spirits would come and tell me different things about, and different approaches to, each person, because each person is different. And what is imprinted on the etheric body of each person is unique to the person's memories of his or her past lives and also unique to the traumas he or she has had, either in this life or in a past life. Therefore, it is never possible for one shamanic session to be equal to another shamanic session. Nothing and no one can prepare you or train you for this, but your courage to put yourself out there to be of service to another human being can.

Shaman-healers are people like everybody else; the only difference is that they have uncovered inside themselves a burning fire of love and a constant wish to serve others, to serve humanity. Every human being has that same fire of love and that same wish to serve others when given the opportunity to overcome basic survival needs. Once you are safe and beyond those needs, you can uncover that burning fire of love and service that is within you.

Reputation is important when choosing a shamanic teacher. The reputation of a good teacher always precedes him or her. Equally as important as good reputation is humbleness and humility. The making of a good teacher is not how much his or her training cost or how long it lasted. Talented teachers are ones who are good at making you feel comfortable emotionally as soon as you meet them. Something in the teacher's aura, something about his or her presence, makes you feel at peace and relaxed. This is because the teacher is at peace and relaxed with himself or herself and holds unconditional love in his or her heart.

Word of mouth is a good source for finding a good teacher. There are some good and some not so good teachers everywhere. Everyone has a different energy, and the amount of self-work the teacher has done, the level of self-mastery the teacher has reached, and the selflessness of the service he or she gives are all a mark of a good teacher. Talk to other people and find out about their experience with any teacher you are considering working with.

A good teacher is one who empowers you, encourages you, and lifts your spirit when you are down. A good teacher is one who will always help you to see that you are great as you are and that you are perfect as you are, and who loves you exactly as you are, without making demands or judgements. Keep away from teachers or practitioners who criticise you or compare you to others, or who push you too hard or want you to walk at a faster pace than you normally do. A good teacher holds and upholds unconditional love at all times and in all situations.

Flexibility of approach is very important. In shamanism, it is not possible to have a template and say that it will serve most of the people. No. That is not possible on the shamanic path. This is because the ancient ways have the flexibility of the wind, and wind has to flow freely. Shamanism is ancient, and yet it has survived because of its flexibility and adaptability. It has survived because no one has been able to put it in a box, mould it, and define it. It survived because it is true and its true nature and approach is flexible. For me, shamanism is like the wind: free, flexible, with no real name, present everywhere, and invisible. It can be very gentle, yet it can also be very powerful and uproot you.

A good teacher looks at where you are and what you are doing in your life and teaches you based on what he or she sees you need, not just from what he or she knows or needs to teach.

Sometimes there comes a point when a student surpasses the teacher, which is the moment a teacher knows he or she has done a good job. This type of situation can be worrying for one as a teacher, but it is ultimately what one really wants: a student who flies out of the nest and flies high up into the sky—and from time to time you catch a glimpse of him or her.

A teacher's ability to adapt and change is one of the hallmarks of a great teacher. In addition, the ability to let projections fall flat on their face is an ability a shamanic teacher acquires over time too. It is important to know that people have a natural way of projection and that as they start to learn, to heal, and to understand, they start to project. They project so they can see and understand what is inside themselves. And because shaman-teachers are human beings connected to the light, it is very common that students will project their dark stuff onto them.

A good shamanic teacher has to be able to work this out and release those projections, be they good or bad projections. This can be hard work. If you do not work on removing those projections constantly, life can become a bit unbearable as it is hard to walk around carrying a lot of that stuff.

I always choose to go back to the mother self. I used to untangle myself from all the projections and labels and tell myself, *I am just a mother like any other mother.* My children have helped me a lot over the years to untie many projections and labels. Now my children have grown up and do not need their mother figure any more. So now I tell myself, *I am just Cláudia.*

It is not easy to remove projections and labels, as they seem to stick to you like superglue does. And when you least expect it, you find yourself wearing them like a coat of armour or some sort of collection of war medals.

Seek a teacher or practitioner who shows consistency in his or her life. Seek someone who practises the healing constantly and consistently and, therefore, can teach others from that place of balance. Teachers such as these will make a deep impact on your life. They reach a deep understanding by practising what they teach.

The best teachers are also lifelong students. They do not see themselves as teachers but as students.

A good teacher is one who motivates you to practise, to live in your day-to-day, the essence of shamanism, communicating with everything around you, learning from everything and everyone around you.

Contrary to what some people think, namely that having the techniques is all you need, in shamanism there are no techniques. The nature and flexibility of this ancient approach often throws out the window all the techniques one knows.

Furthermore, without the help and the teachings of the loving spirits, it is not possible for us shamans to do anything or help anyone. It is because of this that we need to go to do the work with open hearts. We go with loving hearts—and that is all we can do or offer. Then the spirits enter our etheric bodies and hearts to do the work. Without the spirits, we cannot do anything, and without a loving open heart, the spirits cannot enter us to work.

Then comes a point where the spirits become your teacher. How do the spirits begin to be your teacher? They observe you, they read your heart, and they read your aura. Your aura has to be bright; it has to glow in the spirit world for them to see you. How does your aura glow in the spirit world? You keep yourself in alignment with truth and love, you truly love people from your heart, and you truly serve people with a genuine intention to help them. A healthy, positive mind, a loving heart, and a clear, healthy diet can help you have a healthy etheric body. That etheric body will glow in the spirit world.

That is not to say that you do not have outbursts, or that you never feel angry, or that you are never this or that. On the contrary, you feel all of that, because you are a human being like every other human being on this earth. However, you constantly work on yourself. You are constantly chipping away at your sharp edges and constantly looking within. If you can do that, then you are in a good place and are mastering the self.

Once the spirits see you glow, once they see your aura, they begin to pay attention to you. The spirits with healing gifts are always looking for people in the physical realm to partner with. Spirits cannot perform healing in the physical realm without a catalyst, a channel, a person in the middle world who can be that bridge between the worlds. That is where the shaman-healer comes in handy, working in partnership with the spirits.

Without the spirits, the shaman-healer is like every other person: a normal ordinary person. So that makes people confused, because often people are looking for teachers, practitioners, or healers whom they can put on a pedestal, or teachers who put themselves on a pedestal who live saintly lives. Since the shaman-healer is not channelling spirits twenty-four hours a day, some people get disappointed when they see a shaman-healer being a normal human being.

Ultimately, it is my view that, the best and most powerful way to find a good teacher is to look for the teacher within yourself. There is no better teacher than your own guides, your own past life memories, your own ancestral memories, your own self, and your own intuition, remembering your true self.

Merging with Spirits

As you progress in your shamanic practice, at a more advanced stage of your work you will begin to merge with your guiding spirits. The more you work with your community offering healing, the easier this process is. Dedication and perseverance are important. Losing your fears and letting go of blockages that keep you too bogged down in the physical world is necessary.

The loving guiding spirits will never force themselves upon you. They will not take control of your body without your permission. A relationship of mutual support, respect, and deep understanding between you and your loving spirits begins to form. The spirits trust you, and you trust the spirits. Sometimes you may have guides working with you from wherever they are whereabouts unawares. With time, your awareness will expand and you will be able to see as clear as day, like when a light switch is flipped on in a dark room.

When I started working with the spirits, I would usually pray a specific prayer every time I would start a healing session. Over a period of six months to a year, I began to notice there was a certain way of working with energies. I repeated this method with every client I would see. I began to pay attention to this pattern in my work and noticed that there were specific sounds I was making. And as I would clear and cleanse the person, it was as if all that energy then moved into my body and had to be released afterwards. I would automatically start yawning, which I'd continue to do the whole time I was doing the cleansing, until all that energy had moved out of the person's body and out of my body. I noticed that the more I would move my hands or the feather I use around the person's aura to clear and cleanse it, the more releasable energy would move into my body. Depending on how heavy and dark the person's energy field was, this process could take between fifteen minutes and half an hour of work, and sometimes even longer. Then, just like that, I would stop, at which point I'd know that the energy healing work was completed.

What was interesting about this was that sometimes I felt like a dragon blowing fire out of my mouth. It took me a long time to realise that this was a new guide working with me. Soon after the session would end, I would forget all about it. I would forget about the dragon, and I would forget what happened. Then the next person would come in for a healing, and I would experience the same thing. This happened for months and months. In fact, it is still like that to this day. The difference now is that I am aware of my dragon guide and I have given him a space in my personal medicine wheel. Now I can call on the dragon when I need help to transmute energies.

Some people who are more aware can identify new guides straightaway. Other people, like me, are a bit slow or maybe too busy with the physical realm, so we take a long time to see these guides and to reaccess and reorientate ourselves. We are all unique beings working at different paces. It is important to know our strengths and our weaknesses when we work— not to give ourselves a hard time or pile on pressure, but to be patient with ourselves and loving and accepting with ourselves, also accepting the speed at which we work.

When I say I am slow, I mean I am really slow. For example, it took me twenty-two years to completely let go of my fear of merging with spirits. And there is nothing wrong with that. I mean, for the spirits, twenty-two years is the equivalent of two years and two months. However, in human terms, embodied and living in the physical realm, twenty-two years is a relatively long time. Therefore, it was a good thing that I started working spiritually when I was only thirteen years old. Twenty-two years later, at the age of thirty-five, I felt I was ready. Even so, I was as scared as a little mouse feels when it realises for the first time that there are things out there much bigger than it, things out there that can eat it up for supper in one gulp!

When I was thirteen years old, I began to go to a spiritual centre in Brazil to develop spiritually. This was not because I was a highly evolved teenager ready to walk the spiritual path. No, it was because I had no choice. I was a troubled teenager plagued with poor mental health and the desire to die every day. I just could not see the point of being on this earth. As far as I can remember, since the age of five, I was like that. I would cry almost every day, wanting to die. I just did not know how to take my own life. I am pretty sure that if I had known how, I would have done so in no time, which probably would have happened around the age of nine years, when things were really bad. However, my elder Dona Mercedes saved my life. Dona Mercedes was my neighbour. When I was nine years old, my parents moved from the big capital of São Paulo to Mogi-Guaçu, where they still live to this day. Dona Mercedes turned to my mum and said, "This child needs to develop spiritually. This is what her problem is. If I have your permission I will take her to the spiritual centre with me every Friday."

So, for two years, that was that. From the age of thirteen to the age of fifteen, I went to the spiritual centre with my first spiritual teacher, Dona Mercedes, every Friday. In there we would spin like the dervishes do in order to embody our spirit guides. I was terrified at the thought of having a spirit coming into my body. It was more than I could bear. Facing death was an easier prospect to me. However, for those two years I went there, and with time my life began to unfold and make sense. Things began to change slowly; I slowly gained a sense of direction. The thought of wanting to die slowly disappeared, and a more confident and happier teenager began to emerge.

In 1983, at the age of fifteen, I left my parents' home to study and work in Rio de Janeiro. I only returned home, as I still do, at holiday times to visit family and friends. However, at fifteen, I was far, far away from allowing any spirit to enter my body. I was not ready, not then, which is why that spiritual journey took another twenty-two years to unfold. It was only in 2005 that I consciously allowed a spirit to enter my body. I would allow a spirit to be around my energy field, but my fears would prevent it from coming any closer than that. Spirit guides never push a person to go faster than he or she can or force anyone to do something. They always respect our pace and our ways.

When you are a channel for Spirit, or when you are born with the so-called "gift", if you do not have the opportunity to align yourself with the higher-vibrational spirits, then the low-vibrational spirits will quickly find you and plague you. Low-vibrational spirits might well hang around you, and they can make your life quite miserable at times. Their purpose for being there is not always to try to disturb you or cause problems, but because they need your help and they think you can help them. Most people with spiritual gifts are usually sensitive—are empaths—and carry a light within them. Even if it is a very small light, when it is dark out, that little light will illuminate every corner.

The illumination in the darkness will attract the spirits who have lower vibrations and the ones who are stuck in this earthly realm. They will surround the light, you. In some ways you are their only hope and their only light. They do not know that, although you have the gift, you do not yet know how to use it to help them. Little do they know that you need help too. And because of their lower vibration, or the traumas they suffered in their life, or how they died, or their sheer addiction to things or people in this realm, they cannot raise their vibration on their own. They cannot become more than a lower-vibrational spirit, which is the reason why they are stuck here in the first place. When they see your light, they surround you like a plague of locusts in hopes that you will somehow help them. What they do not realise, and what most people do not realise, is that these lower-vibrational beings can cause many energy problems for people in the physical realm.

I see many people for shamanic sessions who have spirit attachment or spirits who sit at the ends of their beds. The fear is so grave for the person seeking healing that it all gets confusing and frightening. Most people think that the spirits are there to harm them, when in fact most of them are there hoping that the people they're attaching to can help them!

For those with the gift, I recommend you begin to learn to journey in order to connect with your spirit guides and power animals that hold a higher vibration and can help you to help the low-vibrational spirits make their passage fully into the light. You may ask why the spirit guides do not do this for themselves. Why are there so many spirits stuck in the earthly realm, and why are the loving guiding spirits not helping them? To answer: because the lower-vibrational spirits need a catalyst, a person in this physical realm who can work as a doorway, a bridge between the physical and the spiritual realms, to help them from this end to do the work.

When the loving guides find someone who carries light within, they know that this light is everything. The light that you carry can help the loving spirits with their work. This is the reason why you will hear the word *channel* being used to describe someone who carries the light. A person who carries this light is very highly regarded by the loving spirits. They need us and we need them, to form a partnership of love. The more light you carry within you through your work of being of service to humanity, through your compassion and loving heart, the more guides will come to work with you.

The vibration and density of the physical realm is too much for the loving higher-vibrational spirits; hence the need for a channel, a person with the gift, a medium, a healer. A shaman-healer who carries a beam of light is essential for the spirits to do their work, in the same way that the spirits are essential for the shaman-healer to do his or her work.

The more you work helping people from a place of service, the more guides come to you. And then more people learn about your work. The more people learn about your work, the more people come to you, and before you know it, they show up with issues they are dealing with that seem more complicated, things that, for you as the healer to help with, will only energise you and strengthen your work.

At the same time, you need to replenish yourself and take rests. Time spent in nature or just going away and doing nothing is important and becomes paramount. When one serves, it is very easy to burn oneself out if one is not constantly keeping oneself in check. When I talk about keeping the self in check, I mean not only checking the ego or shadow, but also checking to see if one is out of balance and needs rest.

I have many stories of spirits being around me which will be either for another book or for telling while sitting around a fire when I am older. I have one I would like to share with you now about when I was travelling in Bolivia in 1992. We took a tour with other tourists, about six or seven of us altogether, with a local guide. We were travelling for quite a while in the direction of Uyuni Salt Flat and Isla Incahuasi in Bolivia, part of which is a beautiful landscape of pure salt. To get there, you drive a whole day sunrise to sunset. You have to sleep over in a little village midway on the journey, with local people who are mostly indigenous. The next day, you proceed with your journey to visit the most astonishing cactus sanctuary, and at night, you are back in the village again to sleep—and then it is another full day traveling to get back home.

The first night, my boyfriend could not sleep—he was visited by spirits all night—while I was so tired that I saw nothing but my pillow that night. The following night, he was going on and on about how uncomfortable he was and how bad everything was. What we were not aware of at that point was that it was spirits who were making him uncomfortable.

I said I would change places with him—terrible mistake! From then on, it was my turn not to sleep. The spirits then began visiting me that night. I was in a suspended place, neither asleep nor awake, the place in between worlds. A little boy about seven years old came to me. He was crying. I saw him trying to pick up something that he could not reach. Touched by his crying, I went to help him. When I lifted him, he wanted to pick up a candle from a cemetery. I put him down again and said, "You cannot have that. That candle belongs to someone in the cemetery." The little boy kept crying and crying, almost sobbing, because he really wanted the candle. I could not understand why. Then another spirit came in. It felt as if a smoky being, an adult—one of this current era in time—was in the room, and was moving frantically in the air. The child was flying behind this spirit, which felt like a woman. The two of them were circulating in the room where all of us were sleeping. The room felt full, and I felt the adult was unsettled, anxious, and stuck.

I was in between worlds, again, neither awake nor asleep. The spirits were keeping me half awake, and I was exhausted. They would not leave. Of course they would not leave, because we were the ones in their space. I could feel their energy and sense their disembodied body flying up and down. The nights when this would happen seemed to be endless nights of exhaustion, both physical and mental exhaustion. An idea came to mind. I said to the mother and child, "OK, please let me sleep, and I promise that tomorrow I will go to the cemetery and light a candle for each of you."

Well, I will say this, if you ever promise something to a spirit, make sure you do it. A promise bounds you to the spirit, and the spirit will be around you for a long time until you do what you promised. Therefore, never promise something that is beyond your capacity to deliver; promise only what you can deliver. This applies to all spirits, including any soul parts you retrieve for someone during a soul retrieval session.

I slept fine after that; things somehow calmed down. In the morning, we were having breakfast with the tour guides, so I asked them in my broken Spanish if someone had died in that room where we stayed that night. One of the guides wanted to know why I was asking such a question. I explained that I had been visited by two spirits at night, a woman and a child, the child around seven years old. He gave a very dismissive answer— the kind of answer that showed me that he assigned little importance to what I had just said. This can happen too. Sometimes when you speak of spirits with people, they do not quite know what to do and therefore will dismiss the subject. When breakfast was out of the way and everyone was packing, the guide went out. He returned with the owner of the house. She wanted to talk to me. She wanted to know more, so I told her my story. Then she told me hers. Her mother had died in that room seven years before, after giving birth to a baby boy. They died of labour complications.

This story tells us that sometimes spirits, depending on the circumstances of their death, can become stuck in between worlds. Although they can see everything in the physical realm, they are not in the physical realm fully, and although they can see everything in the spiritual realm, sometimes they do not have enough power to move to the spiritual realm fully either. Something is holding them in between the worlds. This can be their grief, their pain, their addiction, their sadness, or their sorrows.

After our chat and sharing about what happened, I told the owner of the house that I needed to buy candles and deliver them to the cemetery before our group was to depart. She said she would do that herself. I said no, adding that I had promised them and, therefore, I had to do it myself. We sent her son to buy the candles for me, and she and I walked together to the cemetery.

Sometimes it is not the spirits' own pain, sadness, and sorrows that keep them here, confused. Sometimes it can also be the pain, sadness, and sorrows of members of their family that does that. Their pain too can keep spirits stuck in this physical realm. Every time we grieve, cry over, and call out for a family member who has left the physical realm, we bring that individual back, and he or she may be in between worlds. If the family member is strong enough and holds enough light, he or she can easily return to the spirit world, but if our attachment to the person is very strong, then the darkness of our pain can cloud his or her way and create problems.

CHAPTER 2

Moon Cycle and the Spirits

Women, spirituality, and the taboos that surround woman and spirituality are themes very close to my heart.

I began to notice that at the time of my moon cycle, the people coming to me for healing would present with the most difficult of cases. It was almost as if they knew that I was menstruating and, therefore, it was the best time for them to come. All things and taboos related to menstruation puzzle me, so I am always interested. In many cultures, there is always an aura of mystery, fear, and prohibition related to menstruation, so I have been paying attention to it for a very long time.

It was back in 2004 when I first began to facilitate sweat lodges and began to take note.

I was taught the medicine of the sweat lodge by two very different teachers. For a start, one was a woman and the other was a man. The woman, whom I had approached first, said: "I facilitate lodges when I am in my moon cycle. I have to. I usually have twelve to fifteen people coming, and if it happens that my moon starts, I cannot simply cancel fifteen people." I never questioned that, as it seemed very natural to me what she said.

Then it happened that I had the aforementioned man as my second teacher. More of the old traditional school, he told me, "You must never run a sweat lodge if you are on your moon cycle." Of course, I had to know why! His reply was this: "You follow the old ways. You follow the traditional way that has been done by the indigenous people. This is the tradition, and you must not change or question it. If you are to facilitate sweat lodges, you have to do it the traditional way. There are very specific ways to do it, and you need to respect the old ways." OK, I had no problem with that. But then he said, "A medicine man never enters a sweat lodge with a woman in her moon, because that woman can take his power away."

I began to feel uncomfortable with this; there has never been much explanation about this subject. How can a woman on her moon take a medicine man's power away? For me it felt the reasons were—could be—based on fear.

Not satisfied with the matter of course, my spirit had to investigate further to find my own answers.

I was born a Libra, which means I am only satisfied when I find the underlying cause of things, that is, when I find the truth—the real truth—behind everything. While others may feel satisfied with what they are told, my inquisitive mind always wants to know more and more, so I leave no stone unturned. I am not one of those people who can be happy with half-truth.

I began to research the reasoning behind why women were advised against facilitating sweat lodges when are on their moon cycle. I found many reasons, but the one that felt most truthful to me was that in the old ways, or old times, women were venerated, and the days of a woman's moon cycle was a time to refrain from putting strain on the physical body. It was a time to rest and allow the creative energies to flow through us.

For a while I was satisfied with that answer, and I began to give it as a reason for why the women who were in their moon cycle and wanting to participate in a sweat lodge with me would not be able to do so. However, soon it began to ring as only half a truth to me. So I felt the need to dig deeper. I needed to find out more, as my restless spirit was not satisfied.

The spirits will always find ways to teach you if you are really open to receiving more teachings. Man or woman can only give us half the truth because of the natural limitations we all have as human beings.

So there I was one day, ready to start facilitating the sweat lodge ceremony. The people had arrived. We had carried all the wood and all the stones, had made the fire, and had worked half a day already, when suddenly, without expecting it, my moon began. In my head, immediately the fighting dialogue began: *How am I going to do this ceremony now? How am I going to walk my talk? I have told other women not to come because they are on their moon cycle, and here I am about to enter the lodge and break the rule prohibiting menstruating women from entering the lodge.* Clearly, the spirits created that situation so I could learn some amazing lessons that day, things that no teacher could really teach me.

Against all odds and against the rules, I reluctantly entered the lodge that day, asking the spirits to forgive me and asking the ancient ones who had held this ceremony as sacred to them, very close to their hearts, to protect me and to forgive me for what I was about to do.

When I say that the spirits are my teachers, I mean that they really are. They will make sure I experience everything I need to experience in order to learn and grow spiritually.

I then began to observe to see if there was anything different about that lodge. I noticed that the energies were much stronger. It was as if someone had turned the heat up one level. My sensitivity was enhanced. No surprise there: this is what happens when in my moon cycle anyway, sweat lodge or no sweat lodge. However, I also noticed being swept away quite easily by any of the energies present. I had to be super-vigilant at all times and sieve through all the energies that were passing through me. I was picking up people's emotions and thoughts, their worries and troubles. Of course, no surprise there either. As we women know, this is a very common thing during our moon. However, what was that thing about a woman taking a man's power? What was that about? Does it truly happen?

I began to realise that in that space, if I wanted any one of the men in the lodge to fall in love with me or fall under my spell, as they say, I could make that happen quite easily. All I needed to do was to choose one of them. Thank God, none of them interested me, as I already had my man, but I learnt that day that I could have done whatever I wanted.

Why am I sharing this with you, woman and sister? To tell you that when you are in your moon, you are in your most powerful and energetic time. Anything you put your mind to, you will achieve. However, you must remember to be careful and never abuse that power and create an imbalance. Always use that power wisely.

Why am I sharing this with you dear brother, this knowledge, this experience? To tell you that there is nothing to fear. Venerate and celebrate your woman, respect her, and she will love you to the end for love is women's true nature. Women are open to receiving and giving love.

Why am I sharing this with you, dear medicine man, sweat lodge pourer? Because you are wise beyond your years. It is true that a woman on her moon is very powerful. She will bring you down to your knees, and she will make things energetically difficult for you, but only if you have any flaws within you, any cracks that you are trying to hide or that you are not even aware you have. She will help you open up that crack so more light can come in. Therefore, fear not.

Something else happened in that lodge which proved and confirmed to me how powerful we women are in our moon time. I found out afterwards that another woman entered that lodge on her moon. Inside that lodge, there were a few men, and she picked out one of them. By the end of the session, she had him wrapped around her finger, as the saying goes.

In that lodge I struggled. This I do know. I struggled with my thoughts and my feelings. I struggled with other people's thoughts and feelings, other people's energy. I did not know what was mine and what belonged to others. I wonder if that is what a medicine man feels when a woman in her moon enters his lodge. Does he feel disempowered, unable to move the energy? Does he feel out of control, unable to do his work? If the flow of energy within a woman's body changes in her moon, how much of her energy affects others around her? The flow of the lodge definitely syncs with her flow and it makes it really hard for the lodge pourer.

I learnt one important thing that day: never underestimate the power of a woman on her moon. The power of the Goddess is that she has no fear. The power of the Goddess is to be venerated and worshipped. If you can do that, she will bless you with abundant love.

Years later, amidst my continuous search for truth, I began to wonder why I would get the most complex, traumatic, and difficult cases on the days of my moon. It was a very clear pattern I observed happening for years, which I knew no doubt was happening for a reason. The answer was simple: on the days of my moon, I have more power in my body. My energy is releasing, and I am less distracted because my body slows down, so I am able to focus more. Any trauma or pain I remove from a person is released much more easily when I am on my moon flow, so the work has much more powerful results for the person. My body would be a total wreck after a session while on my moon, but my energy and my senses were super-enhanced. Anything or anyone I would touch, together with my thoughts and feelings, was not short of receiving a miracle if a miracle was what was indeed needed for that person on that day. It was as if people had an antenna and they knew when it was the best time to come see me.

I was happy with my findings and happy that I was on the path of learning, learning directly from Spirit and my experiences in this earthly realm. Until, that is, I went for the Second Ayahuasca World Conference in Acre, Brazil in October 2016.

I was very happy the conference was being held in my country of origin. I figured I would meet new people and my indigenous relatives. I would reconnect more with my indigenous ways. I had learnt a lot from the North American ways, but now I was going back finally to my South American ways. I was overjoyed, until I sat there and heard an academic who studied indigenous people say in his presentation, "The spirits don't like blood. They don't like menstruating women. That is the reason why women are kept separate and away from the spiritual chores." My spirit sank! I felt sad, betrayed, disempowered, and devastated. Yet again, here was a "fact" with a big fat taboo attached to it, with old ways, with rules, and with something about it that did not feel truthful, presented. On my search for truth, I have learnt that truth does not disempower you. On the contrary, truth only empowers. So where was this "fact" coming from? I felt desolated and disempowered as a woman.

My spirit never rests until I learn the truth. I asked myself why, for years of my work, the spirits would bring me the most difficult and traumatic cases only on the days of my moon. Given that they did this, how could it be true that the spirits do not like blood? And, what, spirits do not like menstruating women?

Since that conference in the Amazon, a new guide began to work with me, which I have no doubt is male. He is a very powerful spirit, a power I have not seen before; he speaks an ancient shamanic language. His diagnosis of the problems people present with is spot on. He is a grandfather, wise, serious, truthful, and gentle yet extremely powerful.

I began to notice that on the days of my moon I could not feel his presence as powerfully as I could feel it on the other days. My heart began to sink, and a deep sadness began to overtake me. I thought, *It must be true that the spirits do not like blood. Grandfather is not coming close to me on my moon day.*

However, Grandfather, as all grandfathers do, talked to me and lifted my spirit. He said, "Dear child, it is not that I am not here on your moon days. I am. I never leave you to attend to the sick and the suffering on your own without help. No, that is never the case. It is just that your aura is so big on your moon days and you are so powerful on those days that my powers, compared to yours, become insignificant on those days. Therefore, though you may feel I am not here, but I am here. I would never leave you

34

without help to attend to those in need. As always, I am at the very edge of your aura, which is very big, encompassing all this room. Therefore, you feel as if I am not here. Rest reassured that I am."

Grandfather made my heart sing again. I was very happy to understand that men, academic or not academic, traditional or not traditional, through eyes of limitation, have interpreted the spirits the wrong way.

I felt empowered again. I felt truth had returned and that the divine feminine had once more risen from the ashes in the spot where she burned down. She burned because humankind will always interpret her powers as something to fear, something to burn in the fire, or something to be drowned in the water. The divine feminine will rise higher and higher every time this happens, for the Goddess is not to be feared; she is to be venerated and loved. In her love, there is the balm of healing that will soothe your pain, which will heal your heart. She is your mother, she is your grandmother, she is your sister, she is your lover, and she is all, if only you will allow her in.

I love and honour teachers outside me; however, ultimately, I always go back to the spirits because they are the real teachers.

An excellent book I recommend is *Red Moon: Understanding and Using the Creative, Sexual, and Spiritual Gifts of the Menstrual Cycle* by Miranda Gray.

Spiritual Predators

When people are going through some kind of physical or emotional crisis, they often need someone to talk to, someone who will listen to them, reassure them, and hold them in love. Often they are going through a spiritual awakening, and that awakening usually comes to them as a crisis of some sort, at which time their reality begins to collapse.

In other cases, people are looking for healing from crises caused by the abuse they have gone through. Very often in my work with women I have seen for many years, women who have suffered abuse by so-called "spiritual teachers" from many different spiritual traditions, I have found that these women carry the trauma in their body for a long time—fifteen years, forty years. When they begin to speak of their traumas, the healing process begins. It is very sad and far too common to see men in a position of power as spiritual teachers who misuse their power—without pointing any fingers to any tradition, because the truth is, it happens with all traditions, an unfortunate plague.

Whether the men are not aware of the damage they are doing, or the women are not aware that a spiritual teacher can easily be a predator, this is a place to tread with caution—always.

Sometimes the women are slow to see this kind of abuse; they are already so wounded from past hurts and seeking love that when the spiritual teacher begins to notice them, becomes closer to them, they feel thrilled. They feel they are finally on the path of empowerment, only to find out further down the line that their so-called "spiritual teacher" is actually sleeping around with many women.

I have seen women pay more than two hundred pounds for a shamanic session with a so-called "spiritual teacher", only to end up with an experience that was little more than their being "touched up" by him in a massage session. I see women falling prey to the common sort of predator, someone able to manipulate energy and hook people into his web, reeling them in with personal texts offering sessions, making them feel they are special.

There are too many women who walk around broken and wounded, needing love and needing to be "repaired". That is where a circle of sisterhood can be very helpful. When women come together in a sacred circle, it is like a powerhouse. Masks naturally fall off, we sob together, we embrace one another, and we share things, feelings, thoughts, emotions we never had the courage to share before because we had not found the sacred ground, the supportive ground, we needed.

What we find when in the arms of a lover who takes advantage of our vulnerability and who wounds us is an illusionist, a trickster, or a sorcerer, but never a healer. If that person holds any position as a spiritual teacher, I recommend that my sisters run away. Run as far as you can go from that so-called "spiritual teacher".

I have fallen prey to those predators too—once in my life. I learnt my lesson very quickly. I also learnt what not to be as a teacher. However, that fall required many years of hard work to fix my broken heart. Even after years of gathering my soul back together, I still have a deep scar, which I do not think will ever disappear.

When a woman comes to me for healing, saying she has fallen in love with her teacher or that she had a relationship with her spiritual teacher, I know it will take a long time to bring her soul back to her. For the woman, her heart is broken and her soul has flown away. It takes a long time for such a woman to heal because she does not want those soul parts back. She somehow wants her power to stay with her abuser. She feels that life is not worth living without him, his teachings, his aura, his energy. Those so-called "spiritual teachers" feed on those powers given to them.

Male spiritual teachers who have overinflated egos or who keep sleeping around with their students are usually trying to compensate for one of two things: either a deep childhood trauma or a very small manhood. On both accounts, they need to feel better about themselves.

Today, I can laugh about my experience, but I certainly could not at the time. At the time, I was head over heels, completely caught in my predator's web. It can take many years of hard work to free oneself from such a web and take one's power back.

There are also those spiritual teachers who are like stage hypnotherapists. They can easily hypnotise a whole audience, who do not even realise they are being hypnotised. If you encounter a teacher like this, always keep your hands crossed in front of your navel when you are in his presence. The way in which such teachers get into your energy is through your solar plexus and navel. I always bring my awareness to my navel and solar plexus when I am in the presence of spiritual teachers since I really don't know who is and who is not a predator.

Once I found myself in a hotel helping a Native American medicine man do some healing work for women. The Body and Soul Healing Fair had finished in Aberdeen in Scotland. I had my own stall, where I was offering shamanic healing, back at the beginning of 2002. He had his stall, where he was selling Native American crafts, including flutes. He was booking women to have healing sessions with him after the Body and Soul Healing Fair. When I went over to his stall, he looked at me and probably thought, *Hah, this one will be a good prey today.* I embodied the power of the Goddess; I was young, beautiful, and open. Such men see that power and they want it. He played the Native American flute for me, as it is done in the East for the snake to come out of the basket, hypnotising the creature. The first thing I did was to buy two flutes from him, without even asking the price. He then said he would come to my stall at the end of the day to deliver them. That was that—I was caught in his web. When he arrived at my stall at the end of the day, he charged me one hundred pounds for each flute. All the money I had made that weekend, after paying for my stall, went to him.

Before I had a chance to close my jaw in disbelief, he revealed yet another card heretofore hidden under his sleeve. He asked me if I would assist him with his healing sessions in his hotel room that evening. Eight women had booked to see him, so he needed an assistant. Oh, wow! What else could I dream of? Picture me, helping this totally gorgeous Native American man with long black hair with two feathers in it! How could I possibly be thinking of the two insignificant flutes costing me a mere two hundred pounds when I was actually going to be assisting this amazing medicine man and learning so much from him?

Immediately, I said, "Yes, of course I will. Just give me the address and I will be there. What time would you like me to arrive?" I changed my plans that evening. I had been going to have dinner with a friend who was more, the possible beginnings of a relationship, but now I was to go and assist this Native American man. I said to my friend to come and pick me up at the hotel later. He did not know it yet, but he saved my life that evening when he came.

During the sessions, I was present in the room with each woman. One by one, they came for their healing, which lasted for no more than twenty-five minutes each, yet cost them an absolute fortune, which each had paid to the so called "medicine man" earlier in the afternoon at the Body and Soul Healing Fair. I welcomed them, brought them from the reception to the room, and smudged them. I passed him the drum and his chart, which was using to give him the names of the each women's healing stone and herb name according to her date of birth. He drummed around each woman for a few minutes and gave each the names of her stone and her herb, and that was it. Now I can laugh about how naive I was.

Soon after the sessions had finished, he took me to his room. I knew what was coming to me. I was sexually harassed that night. Things could have been worse if I had not been stronger or not been fully protected by my guides. He began to roll a cannabis cigarette and offered it to me. I said no. Then he began to smoke it. Soon, as he began his sexual approaches, the phone rang. It was my friend at the reception, who had come to pick me up. Luckily, the room was on the ground floor, close to the reception, so all I needed to do was to walk out and I would be safe.

I put my coat on and reached the door, but to my dismay, the key was not there. The door was locked and the key gone. He knew it was too late now for my friend was at the door and knew where I was. He hadn't known someone would be coming to pick me up. He had no option but to give me the key for the door. As it is with my warrior guides, they always find a way to rescue me. I was lucky to have escaped.

Today, nearly twenty years later, I look back at this story and think, *How on Earth did I fall for that? How naive could I possibly have been?*

However, experience is everything. Every experience teaches me something. After that experience, I had two more so-called "spiritual teachers" in my life whom I immediately identified as predators, teachers who manipulate energy, those who can hypnotise a whole audience without the audience even noticing it, preying on the weak—preying not only on women but also on anyone who is too open or susceptible, anyone who can easily become one of their followers. I have seen this happen many times in North and South American indigenous cultures, the use of medicine to lure people in. For me, this is abuse of power.

Nowadays, there are those who have the ability to lure people in via social media—an even more cunning use of energy. A user simply looks into the eyes of the so called "teacher" in his or her profile picture, and that's enough. The spirits call teachers like this *soul eaters*, but that is another topic for another day.

Suffice to say that it is important to remember that people such as those just described are not medicine people; they are sorcerers. And one needs to know how to distinguish between a shaman-healer and a sorcerer—like identifying which plants in your gardens are weeds and which are not. The earlier you are able to identify them, the better. Sorcerers manipulate energy and play with power, which they use to get what they want. And usually they want followers who give them money and energy. There are so many walking around out there consciously looking for prey. If you do not have enough power, you can easily fall prey to them. *They are wolves in sheep's clothing.* They usually present themselves as great teachers, powerful shamans; they are there to rescue you! They have no mercy; they need your energy, and they will drain the light out of you.

I would say, always be aware of your core, your navel, in the presence of such teachers. And do remember that sorcerers can be male or female.

Luckily, nowadays, it is quite easy to suss people out and find out if their work is genuine thanks to the internet and social media. However, it is also important to remember that many spiritual teachers refrain from using their own names. Often they change names or relocate as another way not to leave behind any traces of their dark past. So always check if a teacher you feel drawn to has a history. If there is no history, it might be because they changed name in order to erase their dark past.

If all else fails, follow your intuition, your gut feeling. If you have protected your navel and solar plexus in the presence of such a teacher, then it is unlikely that he will have used his or her power to remove your intuition from you, which is the first thing such teachers attempt to do. I always trust my first gut feeling about someone. Sometimes I simply do not click with the person. I can find no reason for that, but I always trust my instinct. It is as if my extra senses are telling me, *Do not go there,* so I simply do not go there. No explanation, no reason, just a feeling—and that is enough for me to keep my distance.

If someone comes to me bringing that kind of problem, namely lost power or having had their power stolen, I go into the spirit world to bring the power back for them. If the person is empowered enough, I guide him or her into the spirit world and with his or her helpers, and together we retrieve the person's power. Often, when people come to you complaining that their power has been taken away, they will need you to intercede and do the work for them until they are powerful enough to do it themselves. I usually teach people how to bring their own power back. ceremony is one of the most powerful ways to bring one's power back.

Going back to the story earlier in this chapter, I'd like to tell you what happened with regard to the amazingly good-looking Native American. Well, years later, my husband read in the newspapers that a well-known Native American had been through the courts accused of sexual assault, following a series of accusations of sexual harassment up in the north of Scotland, in Aberdeen. It was found that he also had a similar history back in his home country. That is the good news. The bad news is that those types change names, change countries, and often change the way they look too.

To finalise my thoughts on spiritual predators, I would encourage my sisters to sit in women's sacred circles together. I also highly recommend Laura Moreno's work *Mujeres que Despiertan* (Women Awakening). In this work, women meet in sacred circles to awaken and empower themselves. There are more than two hundred women's awakening circles around the world, and the number keeps growing. Our beautiful Colombian sister Sylviana Geoffray, who now lives in Quebec, Canada, has translated the work into English, which means that even more women around the world will be able to run the groups. Laura is always looking for people to translate the work into their language, so women who are interested in empowering women should contact Laura Moreno in Colombia and begin to facilitate women's awakening circles wherever they are in the world. The work is voluntary, which is a wonderful thing.

For our brother who would like to sit in a sacred circle of brothers to empower and be empowered, Laura Moreno also offers *Hombres que Despiertan* (Men Awakening). Laura Moreno is from Colombia, as mentioned, but she travels all over the world with her work. You can find her on social media too. In Scotland, my husband Mark Halliday, runs men's circles too, a place for brotherhood, support and healing.

Crises, Spiritual Call, and Family

When I started to work with people shamanically in Scotland in 2001, my children were very small. My daughter was eighteen months old, and my son was five years old. They were all I had. My life was dedicated to them and to the work of Spirit.

At the end of 2002, Mark Halliday suddenly appeared in our lives. I felt he was a gift brought by the spirits to love me and support me and, in turn, for me to love him and support him. To this day, I still ask myself, *What have I done to deserve such a loving, dedicated, and selfless man in my life?* Like every couple, we have our ups and downs, but most of the time

42

our life is balanced, right in the middle, no ups and no downs. This gives us a peaceful life, a life we enjoy together. Our love serves not only us but also our community and those who seek our counsel. The gifts that Spirit has bestowed on us in our sacred union as man and woman, we share with others.

We have no children of our own, but we have two children from my previous marriage whom Mark took on as his own, helping me to raise them and providing a safe haven for their upbringing and empowerment. Today, my children are happy and balanced adults. Both have a deep sense of purpose and are strongheaded young adults. Like me, they speak their mind; they are truthful and sensitive human beings. I owe to this family all my happiness, and I thank Spirit every day for bringing them into my life.

My second spiritual call came to me in the year of 2001, when I was thirty-three. As it is with every spiritual call, this one came to me in the form of a life crisis.

I was married and had two young children. I was so unhappy that I became suicidal. As I have had a history of never really wanting to be in this world, this feeling was a familiar one to me. Nothing I had accomplished or acquired in this life, not my academic titles or material possessions, seemed enough to make me happy. I did not feel any joy, and on top of that, my marriage was failing. The only thing that kept me here were my children, the sense of duty I had towards them, and the fact that they were very young and still needed me.

What helped me to carry on was my connection with Spirit. My life is full of connection with the unseen world, with a higher force which I call Spirit. This force is beyond me and is beyond this physical reality. It is a force I cannot explain to you, but I know it exists and guides me. Spirit takes me by the hands, just like a parent takes a little child, and teaches me all I need to know. Spirit opens my heart and my eyes every day to see the beauty of life around me.

Blessed has my life been ever since I accepted this force that is beyond me. Many people who have come into my life have mirrored Spirit to me. A sense of purpose and Spirit has filled me. I know where I am going, and I enjoy every step I take. I take the time to breathe in, all around me, the beauty of nature where I live and everywhere I go, enjoying the peace of the countryside, my loving family, and now my spiritual families at the Planetary Healing Centre, the Edinburgh Shamanic Centre, and Youth Vision, along with the indigenous people back home.

So it is that I have filled my life with purpose. Although Mark and I have not had a child together, we have had many projects that are our children. These keep us busy, on our toes, all the time. We live a happy life filled with Spirit and people, as well as two cats and a dog. Our life is truly full of love and joy.

We serve day and night, we serve at weekends, we serve weekdays, and we serve when we are on our holidays too, none of which is a burden. On the contrary, it is pure joy. We create love around us, and that love is contagious, like the hummingbird and the butterfly in our logo, with their tireless flapping of wings and kissing of flowers.

Somehow we have found a balance too. Through our imbalances we found a balance. In extremes, we have found our centre.

When my children were very young, I was learning to integrate my spiritual life with my family life. Many times I cried to Spirit, saying I could not do spiritual work and do family life. The answer I would get from Spirit was always the same: "There is no separation between your family life and your spiritual life. They are one and the same." It took me many years to fully understand what that means. Today my children are adults, as I've said; and only now I am beginning to understand what Spirit meant.

Our crises are the opening for Spirit to come in. Our family is the container, and our community, is where we can truly practise our spiritual life.

Spirit Attachments and Extraction Work

How does one identify if a person has an intrusive energy? Quite often, people come for a shamanic session complaining that they have a spirit attachment or feel something is stuck to them, or that someone is following them or observing them. Sometimes they feel something is attached to their back or attached to the back of their head, or that something is lingering around. Other times, they feel energies moving around their body, like tiny snakes, causing discomfort or pain.

I usually ask people if sometimes they catch themselves having inappropriate thoughts, having inappropriate behaviours, or thinking suicidal thoughts. These are all signs of what we call spirit attachments.

That brings us to ask a few questions: Where do spirit attachments come from? What is their purpose? Why do spirits linger around people?

Sometimes these spirit attachments are disembodied souls who have not managed to fully complete their passage into the spirit world. Most of the time, they are lost without direction. Other times, they are aware they have died but are not ready to complete their passage and want to stay here. These spirits who do not want to leave the earthly realm are a bit more difficult to work with. However, *difficult* does not mean impossible; it just means more power will be needed to do the work. For example, if they are spirits whose consciousness has not developed enough, or if they were people with very negative lower vibrations, or indeed if they do not have enough power to complete their passage, they will linger around and will not want to leave.

However, there are also some who do not even know that they no longer have a body. These spirits stay in houses and other places for a long time, trying to have a normal life as it was before they died. However, things are not the same. Other people have moved into their home, or their loved ones are no longer there. Besides, their loved ones might have died as well or moved house. Time has passed, yet these spirits do not realise it.

This kind of thing is a very common occurrence. Sometimes all these spirits need is reassurance, acknowledgement, and help from someone who is sensitive enough to "see" them and explain things to them, someone who is able to help them make their transition. They are the simple cases to deal with because all the shaman-healer is doing is helping someone in need.

There is also another, very different scenario, and that is when we are dealing with souls who do not want to make that transition or passage. They could be addicted to things in the physical realm. For example, if they have had an alcohol addiction before, they linger around people who drink alcohol. If they were psychologically addicted to cannabis, they will stay around people who smoke cannabis. If they were addicted to sex, they linger around people who can give them that thrill. If they enjoyed material things in the physical world, it might be hard for them to let go and leave possessions behind. These souls know very well where they want to stay, and that place is here. In this case, there has to be a bit more of, let us say, ruthlessness from the shaman-healer in order to move these spirits to the other side and close the door. As a shaman-healer, you need to connect to your inner bouncer, as this work is a bit like throwing someone out of your home who has been drunk and sneaky, causing nonsense and big problems. You, as the shaman-healer, need power for that. My husband Mark Halliday is really good at that kind of work. I have seen him on numerous occasions working with souls that do not want to leave. You need to impose respect and bring order. You need to be serious, accepting no nonsense and doing whatever you need to do to restore peace.

I would say that only a very small percentage of spirits are like that and do not want to leave the earthly realm. The majority are just spirits stuck in between dimensions, mostly needing help and direction to leave the earthly realm.

We cannot underestimate what spirit attachments can do to us in the physical realm, as any spirit stuck, whether it wants to be here or not, can cause us a great deal of energetic problems. People have experienced weakened energetic bodies, confusion arising from the spirit's confusion, and anger or rage, because these spirits can also be angry or raging.

Long-term spirit attachments can also cause physical problems in people. Sometimes doctors try to sort out problems that people present to them, doing tests (including blood tests), scans (including MRIs), endoscopies, and so on, yet they cannot find anything wrong with the person. If you are in a situation like that, it is a good idea to get yourself checked by a shaman-healer because the problem may be an energetic one or a spirit attachment. Spirit attachment is more common than we think. I would say, always check with your doctors first. If they cannot find a problem, that is if nothing is wrong with you, yet you are experiencing disturbance, then your problem may be an energetic one.

Nowadays, more and more people die a sudden death by way of accidents, disasters, or other unexpected traumatic occurrences. When that is the case, because of the shock, the affected soul does not always manage to complete its journey to the spirit world. Souls like this need help. Sometimes they linger around spiritually gifted people, but sometimes it happens that gifted people do not know how to help these lost souls. Sometimes people think they are cursed because they attract spirits, but this is not the case. The ability to see in the spirit world is an amazing gift. Sometimes we just need to accept the gift and develop it like we do any other gift.

Sometimes I have the feeling of someone hanging around my house. Do you know that feeling you have when it seems that someone is watching you or following you? Well, that feeling arises because someone *is* watching you and following you. The spirit needs you to open the doorway of the spirit world for it, show it the way, so it can pass. All we need to do is stop for a moment, light a candle to illuminate the path on the other side so the spirit can see, and then open the door to the spirit world with a prayer. Through that prayer, we call our loving guides to take the spirit and guide it safely to the other side. Sincerity, unconditional love, and service to another being is all that is needed. Love is all that is needed for this work. It is a bit like someone stopping you on the road when you are rushing for a meeting and you are late, and this person asks you for directions, where to go and how to get there. When you stop your physical life and give a bit of your time to help another being, you create balance and harmony around you. Everyone benefits, you, your family, and the lost soul.

Sometimes when we do spiritual work from home, our space becomes a beam of light, a lighthouse, and sometimes souls will come, attracted by that light. In the hopes of help, they come towards the light.

If you begin to see lost spirits or spirit attachments as children who have lost their way and need help, this will make it much easier for you to overcome the fear of spirits. You can then begin to work with these souls and guide them home, for they are children who are trying to go home.

When you see or feel the presence of a spirit, there is no need for fear or panic. Just go to the spirit and ask lovingly, "Can I help you?" Nine times out of ten, the spirit is hoping that someone will help it. Most of the time we find ourselves too busy with our daily lives to pay attention even to the real people we encounter, so how can we pay attention to the invisible people? How can we pay attention to the invisible world, which most people do not even believe exists and which no one can see? Well, at least the majority of people cannot see it. The spirit world is like air. One's not being able to see it does not mean it does not exist.

Now, when it comes to spirit attachments, the weaker the energy field within a person, the more a spirit can control that person's mental thoughts. Mental health institutions would benefit from having the same number of shaman-healers working as they have doctors on the ground. People with mental health issues either started having mental health problems because of spirit attachments or attracted spirit attachments because of chemical imbalances leading to poor mental health.

Sometimes you clear the spirits out just to find out that other spirits come in. Therefore, people with mental health issues sometimes benefit from having their crown chakras closed slightly for a little while after receiving a good cleansing and after having their energy body balanced. Why is that? Because they are so open spiritually that it is very difficult for them to control all spirits who seek either help or a thrill.

Every person with mental health issues would benefit from developing spiritually and learning to have their own guides working with them. Learning how to open energetically and how to close down energetically and not be at the mercy of spirits is fundamental for good mental health.

It is not easy to work with people with mental health issues. They are constantly in crisis and often do not know boundaries. You need to be energetically strong to work with them. It is like taking someone who is drowning out of the water. If you are not quite sure what to do and how, you can easily drown with the person you're trying to help. Love, compassion, and patience with the person—and with oneself—are essential.

Most of the time, people's mental health crises happen because they are overwhelmed with the spirit world. They experience such intensity in their feelings and emotions that it becomes turmoil.

Hearing spirits, seeing spirits, and feeling spirits around us is more common than we imagine. There is nothing to fear. Just see each of those spirits as someone needing help. Open the doorway to the spirit world and show them the way. Sometimes they need healing, too, before they go. For example, they might need closure and resolution of things in the physical realm first before they leave. When the situation is like that, we acknowledge it, help the spirits to do that healing, and then show them the way.

Sometimes my guides will come and take some spirits to a realm of learning, a place where, if they were not good people in this physical realm, they choose to stay and cause problems. When that is the case, a *falange* of spirits, a group of good spirits, come to take them away as if taking a prisoner away. Those spirits have no choice but to go with the falange to learn a better way of being.

Those kinds of spirits are not ready to enter the pure realm of spirit because they could cause problems in that realm too. Therefore, they have to go with the falange of spirits to a place where they will first learn some good ways and some good manners before they are ready to enter the realm of pure spirit.

For the spirits who are just lost and confused, I have the hummingbird that takes them to the spirit world. The vibration of hummingbirds is of pure love and service. Hummingbirds, like angels and fairies, are very happy to help.

As for the spirits who stay, knowing they are still in the physical realm and are here to cause problems, I count with a group of spirit helpers who come to take them away. These are like warrior spirits. They are strong, they have a great sense of authority about them, and they are the type that no one, embodied or not embodied, would ever dream of messing with.

The best way to do extraction work is to count with all your power animals and spirit helpers. Sometimes people may have three, four, or more spirit attachments, each one causing a different problem.

Sometimes, people get so used to the spirit attachments that when you actually remove them, they go into some form of energetic crisis. Some people have terrible physical symptoms such as diarrhoea; others may get very ill for a day or two. Some have withdrawal symptoms, a bit like going cold turkey. All we can do is reassure the person that it will pass, because it will. The energy will balance itself out and life will carry on, but life will be very different—for the better.

I cannot stress the importance of, after doing an extraction work, actively rebalancing the person's energy field. Feather Stone Energy Healing work is perfect for rebalancing the energy field. Extraction work is a bit like removing a big stone from the bottom of a pond. The water will get a bit upset, and a bit of mud will mix with the rest of the water, but eventually things will settle down again.

Extraction work is one of the most fascinating works in shamanism. As a practitioner, one either hates it or loves it. It has taken me many years to get used to this kind of work. I think one needs to do more and more of it in order to get used to it.

Then you have the alien types and the lizard types that attach themselves to people in the earthly realm. These are sometimes described as beings from other realms. Somehow, at some point, if the doorways between worlds are left unattended, these beings find their way here to the physical realm of humans.

We must not give our power away to them. We must not think of them as good or bad. They just are. And their realm is not the earthly realm, so the best way is just to send them back to where they came from. Give them no thought or power.

Then there are the spirits of family member and loved ones that people sometimes call to this realm. My belief is that unless the spirits we are calling are ancestors, there is very little they can help us with in this realm. If they are ancestors, as such, they will have accomplished a great deal of work and learning on this side and on the other side before becoming ancestors, and therefore they will have a lot to teach us. However, if they have only just recently passed away, they have not yet had time to learn anything in the spirit world which they can share with us and teach us in this physical realm. It is good to give them time.

Ancestors have done their passage a long time ago. With time—I must emphasise, a very long time—they earn their place as ancestors after they have done a great deal of learning in the spirit world. So when we need help, they come to help. They are able to find their way in and out of our world, just as shaman-healers are able to find their way in and out of their world, without getting lost or stuck.

It is important to remember that when family members pass into the spirit world, they have things to learn on the other side. So I would say, only call them when you really, really need help. Otherwise, you'll be like a needy child calling spirits who are your family members, asking for everything you need that you can actually do yourself, not understanding that spirits too are busy and have work and learning to do on the other side.

Deepening Our Nature Connection

Whenever I can and as much as I can, I go and spend time with a beautiful sister across the bridges in Fife. Her name is Adele Clarke. We have known each other for many lifetimes. She is the full embodiment of the Earth Mother. We have seen each other grow spiritually, and we have helped each other with the work.

A day with Adele is full, with magic interwoven with gold. Adele has had many teachers, amongst whom are Don Americo Yabar and Jon Young. Her work is a tapestry made of the best things she has learnt from many beautiful teachers along the way, in addition to her own remembering. Her soul is deep rooted and connected—fully—to the people and the earth. She remembers who she is and helps others remember who they are, including their birthright, their connection, and their sense of belonging. She loves people and our Earth Mother.

A teacher of the art of mentoring, nature connection, and deep nature connection, Adele is helping humanity to recreate a culture that provides reconnection to the earth and full self-empowerment.

Sometimes, one of the things she asks you when you meet her is, "What are you grateful for?" Then she may have you lie on your belly to release. With your belly button touching the earth, you feel held, so you feel you can let go. Sometimes it is not just about release; sometimes you need to receive, so you also open yourself up to receive what our Earth Mother has that she wants to give to you. Other times you are asked to hold a piece of green from the earth, and Adele tells you to hold your breath. Hold your breath for a very, very long time. How does it feel for you? What is life trying to tell you?

When holding my breath, I realise that everything around me wants me to be alive. I *am* loved unconditionally, I *am* accepted, and I *am* included. Nature wants to keep me alive, and life force flows through me unto others and from others to me.

Lying down with my belly touching the earth, I let the Mother know that I want to serve; I want to serve the Mother if she will take me to be one of her helpers. Then the Mother gives me new ideas for our Deepening Our Nature Connection project, but she empties me first. I need to be empty first in order to let something else come in. So, through my belly button, which is touching her, Mother empties me, then fills me with inspiration, new ways to serve.

Sometimes Adele asks you what is it that reconnects you to the quiet mind, what reconnects you to deep listening?

I search deep inside, and the answer comes clear: "When I give to myself and when I take the time to be with myself."

Then she may ask, "Are you able to give your full attention to others? Is your attention filled with initiative, vision, purpose, reverence? Can you come to that place in your life where you know you have everything? What reconnects you to compassion and love?" Then, you search deep, searching to the depths of your being. To give a true answer is to reconnect and re-empower yourself. Mother Earth is there to support you and to guide you to the depths of yourself as you search for the truth, searching for your true self.

Then, Adele asks you to sit with the universe and tell the universe what you are trying to do with your life. It helps when there is no resistance. You can also ask the trees and the grass to give you the answers, and they will.

For me, what keeps me connected to stillness and quietness inside? When I stop the world and give to myself. In that magic moment, something big happens. A gap opens up, and I am able to enter that gap and stay for hours and hours. I rest, I contemplate, I write, I am creative. All of this is possible because my healing is taking place in that moment. I am tending to myself, spending time with myself. When I stop the world and begin to stay with myself, a deep connection forms. I begin to find stillness and a sense of deep connection within, and a deep connection with nature naturally unfolds.

I spend too much time being busy and doing. I spend time with other people's stories, and I create stories too, but when I spend time in nature, I spend time with myself—my own self. Only then does balance return within.

How can I hold unconditional love for another when I am not able to hold unconditional love for myself? How can I hold unconditional love for another and myself in a way that is nurturing, sustainable, kind to the earth, kind to others, and kind to myself?

A day with Adele Clarke is a day filled with love and connection to our Earth Mother, to ourselves and others.

Feather Stone Energy Healing: Four Aspects of Healing

What you are about to read is a description of a short demonstration Mark and I do in our Feather Stone Energy Healing training. We teach many different ways to work with energy in our courses. One of these ways is described here.

With the power of unconditional love in this work, we bring in the guides, aided by the feather and the stone, to restore balance to the client.

The initiation of the Feather Stone Energy Healing works in multiple dimensions and on multiple levels. The energy healer shares unconditional love through that work with the people and the world.

Above is the feather; below is the stone. We work with that vertical axis. Unconditional love is in the centre. Unconditional love sits on the horizontal axis, working on this physical dimension with people, yet it can reach all directions and all dimensions.

There are four aspects of healing: release, cleanse, balance, and restore.

First we open a sacred space; we call our guides and the guides of the person we will be working with.

Release

We pick up our sacred stone and use it to massage the forehead and the temples. We brush and sponge down the temples. We use the flat of the stone to brush down the energy. Many judgements people have get stuck in the hair, so we can use the stone to clear those judgements too.

Stress is the number one enemy of health. Stress creates blockages and causes premature cancers, heart problems, and overstressed brains. With the stones, we remove the stress and work on creating new pathways.

People who have lived stressed lives get dementia earlier. Physical farmers who live a life connected to nature have less of an incidence. People who live very stressful lives are at greater risk of developing Alzheimer's disease, Parkinson's disease, and dementia. So it is important to keep the brain relaxed.

Working with the stones to clear stress from the energy body can help one to return to a place of balance.

We absorb all the heavy vibration of the city through our eyes, so in a session with the feather stone, we can use the stones to clear the eyes by moving the stones around the eyes. We can brush the cheeks with the stones, pass the stones around the mouth and throat, and clear out energetic blockages from these areas with the stone.

After the head is done, the stone can be used like a Brillo pad or a sponge. Going around the energetic body with the stone, imagine you are clearing a black pot, cleaning all that needs to go.

We can do this work on ourselves, or we can work with other people. We can stay awhile at the solar plexus, massaging it gently. By doing so, we are going deeper and deeper into the many layers of consciousness.

Cleanse

We have layers of past lives, layers of trauma. Every trauma makes an imprint on our energetic body, our soul. The spiral is a vortex of healing and is a natural spiritual healing symbol. Every spiritual tradition uses spiral healing. The Celtic stones have spirals on them. The galaxy is spiralling in on itself. Our DNA is shaped like a spiral. When we are using spirals in our healing work, we are creating healing. In the heart, we can create spirals with gentle massage or with the feather. We can also create spirals of healing energy to clear our thoughts by using the stone or the feather.

We can create a point star in each chakra by using the feather as if we are doing an opening. By using the feather like a spoon, we can remove any blocked energy from the chakras.

Lightly tapping the feather in the chakras will bring that which is unconscious into consciousness. We are pulling out *Hucha* (heavy energy), cutting any wormlike energies that we see; we cut these out of the client's energy field. Opening each chakra allows us to go much deeper.

Then we move to the heart. With intent, we open that chakra. We then spin the feather around and remove anything there that is not serving the person anymore.

When the heart chakra is open and then cleansed, we can also put a stone in there and ask the stone to balance and harmonise the heart centre.

When we are working with the solar plexus, we can cut attachments in there and can energetically do a deep cleansing in the solar plexus.

Balance

Like a wheel, our energy centre goes deep inside. We can fill this centre with health, with wheels of light. When we put the stone in there with clear intent, the stone will naturally help restore that centre.

When we are working with the Feather Stone Energy Healing, there are three ways to do hands-on healing:

1. By externally channelling life force to a person's body.
2. By bringing your guides into your body to do more work.
3. By just being the Divine and bringing that energy into your body and channelling it to the other person.

Restore

When we are working with a client, we can ask Spirit to bring down what that person needs. With the palms facing up, we call the energy to come through our hands. We must stay in a relaxed state, bringing our hands down and allowing the energy to flow through us, keeping the intent of seeing the person healed already in our spiritual eye. We then visualise the person in front of us being happy and healthy. Healing energy is never heavy or dark, but always light. We feel it as warmth. There is a warm flow to it.

To channel the energy, we call our spirit guides to come around us. Our guides will come and pull things out of the client's energetic body. When you know and feel that everything in the cosmos is healing and love, then everything around you becomes healing and love.

Then we ask for the energy that the client needs, not what the person wants with his or her mind, but what he or she *needs* spiritually. That energy will come through us to the person; we simply channel the energy for the person. For example, we might get the energy of a pine forest and/ or the energy of birds. We simply let that energy flow to the client. The antibacterial aspects of the pine might be what the person needs, or the birds, or the energy of nature in general. Sometimes you can get colours; other times you might get sound. Each person is different, so each will need something unique to him or her.

In terms of the art of transformation, transforming and turning the muddy water into clear water. We can use the feather to clean up the water. The power is in us to do it. Our ancestors knew how to do it. So do we. We are remembering.

After a cleansing and balancing, it is very important to return the chakra to how it was before.

With the feather, we can finish off by fanning down the body. Tapping the feather is also a good way to bring the client back.

We then thank the energy and close the space in the same way we opened it.

Then we give the person some feedback. We can tell them about the work we did. To finish, we close the sacred space and release all the guides who came to help.

CHAPTER 3

Misappropriation, Misconception, Misunderstanding

The sweat lodge ceremony is considered traditional to the North American indigenous people, but today it is performed all over the world. The same is true of the vision quest, the sacred peace pipe ceremony, and other ceremonies specific to North America. Ceremonies that once *belonged* to certain people now seem to be everywhere around the world.

The same is happening with the Ayahuasca ceremony, which is a tradition passed down from all the Amazonian people of Central and South America. Very much the same as with the other ceremonies, today we find Ayahuasca ceremonies everywhere in the world.

Naturally, there are a lot of discussions regarding misappropriation, that is, wrong or right use of medicines or traditions that belong to others.

This is a very controversial and sensitive subject to talk or write about. It is my personal view that those who are the "originators" of the tradition and those who are "borrowing" the tradition hold a piece of the truth. In any given situation, both sides hold a part of the truth. However, for one to discover the truth, one has to be able to hold both points of views at one time, in other words, walk in another's shoes.

To help find the truth, we need to ask ourselves a question: Why do white people need to use indigenous traditions, performing ceremonies which "belong" to others?

We talk about healing humanity and healing our relationship with the earth. The answer to the foregoing question is simple and clear: The white people need powerful medicine to heal. The white people do not have the medicine they need; therefore, borrowing medicine sometimes is necessary—not to abuse the medicine, but to use it for healing.

We are all able to share. It is in our nature. We all came here to share. Mother Earth is constantly teaching us, her children, to share all the time: she teaches us to share the air we breathe, she teaches us to share knowledge and discoveries, and she teaches us to share the natural resources she gives to us freely.

Some children do not like to share, but our Mother keeps teaching us the art of sharing. Because it is a mother's job, she will teach us to the very end. One day we will learn to share, even if it will be sharing the earth our bodies will be buried in after we take our last breath.

The indigenous people have suffered and still suffer. Some indigenous warriors are very strong and powerful people. Their spirits came here to put right what is wrong. That is their strength and power. However, talking about and labelling some misappropriation is not the only way to make right what is wrong. There are many ways to do that, and sharing medicine is one of those ways.

White people need powerful medicine to heal their wounds, pains, and greed, the kind of medicine that only indigenous people have. So why deny the medicine to one in need? We need to focus on the people who genuinely want to learn the old ways from indigenous people.

If people are misusing the medicine, it is because they have not yet had the opportunity or the good fortune to encounter good teachers to teach them. So let us bring those teachers out, indigenous and non-indigenous, and let us teach humanity the way to use sacred medicine. Let us all change our focus from seeing only the wrong to seeing the right—change our attention from the negatives to the positives. This change in focus will make a huge difference to humanity's ever-evolving consciousness.

We also need to move beyond separation of races, as times have changed and all our suffering has made us into one race: the race called humanity.

Seeking What Is Within

When you are working shamanically, spirits will check what you have in your mind and in your heart. If there is any shadow of doubt within you, the spirits will go away. You have to be very strong and you need to have no doubt when you are working shamanically.

Sometimes the spirits will come and will sniff around the person you are working with. They also check your client's sincerity. They check if the person is worthy of their time and concern. They check if the person is sincere about what he or she wants, needs, or says.

When you are walking the shamanic path, the spirits know what is in your heart as the shaman-healer. They, in fact, know what is in everyone's heart.

The more love you carry within you and the more spiritual work you do with people, the more people will come. The work changes all the time. From time to time, when you are ready, the spirits will decide to open up new layers of teaching to you. The spirits are your teachers, not people in the physical world.

If you are patient and if you hold love in your heart, you will always be presented with new teachings. Holding love in your heart makes space for more love to come in.

If you hold grief, jealousy, sadness, sorrow, anger, or hatred, you need to clear that from your heart first. Make space for love to come in and go out. Only then will the spirits give you new teachings, new learning, new experiences. You need to be patient; the spirits decide when you are ready to receive the gift they have to bestow upon you.

We Need Elders in Our Lives

I cannot remember a time when I wanted to be on this earth. For as long as I can remember, I've had the thought that I didn't belong here. I had no idea why I had landed here; Planet Earth never felt like home. I was never happy and always longed to go home. When I was age five, I left my parents' home to return to where I came from. I desperately wanted to go home, that is until I met an elder.

I was nine years old when my parents moved from the big city of São Paulo to the outskirts of it, a little town called Mogi Guaçu, where they still live today. Mogi Guaçu, which in Tupi-Guarani mean "big snake", is the name of the big river that crosses the town. There I met my elder Dona Mercedes, who then became my spiritual teacher. She was a grandmother who walked the spiritual path of service to others. To this day, I often feel her spirit coming through my work. She held the light for me and allowed me to safely navigate the darker times of my early teenage life.

Sometimes with some genuine elder teachers whom we meet in human form in this physical realm, we tend not to perceive them as guides, but they are also guides. Some are more than just teachers.

True teachers hold the light for you without making a fuss, without blocking your path or interfering with you. They just *are* in your life and make sure you are safe and held in love.

When Dona Mercedes died twenty years after I first met her, I felt a great sense of loss in the physical world, but at the same time, I knew she would continue to guide me, inspire me, and work with me in this physical realm and beyond.

Another great teacher appeared in my life in 1992, two years before I came to the United Kingdom. His name was Elviro. From the tribes of the Amazon, he was one hundred and four years old. He helped me to begin looking within to *see* who I am and to find my gifts, the gifts that the universe had given me. My son bears the name Elviro as his middle name, in honour of Elviro's life.

Today I honour the elders around me. They are advisers in our charity. Alma Shearer, Stewart Keith, Emily Boyd, Jed Pemberton (in memory), and Margot Daru-Elliot, all in their seventies and eighties, have all served in our Planetary Healing Centre charity as members of the board of trustees for nine years, and after their retirement as trustees, they became our council of elders in person and in spirit.

Grandmothers Dorothy Forest, Ann Fowler, Tessa McKirdy and Sue Tait are volunteers at the Planetary Healing Centre, giving to the community without expecting anything in return. They give off the true essence of an elder's unconditional love and compassion.

Another beautiful elder in my life is Margaret Harper, whom I often visit. One of the things I like about Margaret is her truth. Elders see through you. They see your pain, your flaws, your sadness, and your sorrows, but equally, they see your power and your light.

If you don't know who you are, ask an elder to tell you, as they see the whole entirety of you. Elders always enrich our lives with their generosity, patience, unconditional love, knowledge, and wisdom, and their beam of light illuminates our path.

I highly recommend that you surround yourself with elders. Begin to know them, learn about their life stories, and tell them your life story. Elders have a lot to give, especially to the young people in our society.

To Awaken to the Proper Use of Our Spiritual Power

There are those of us who are walking a path—be it spiritual, or connection to the self or to nature, or the healer's path, any path really on the human path—who are constantly called to deeper places within

63

ourselves. To gain the ability to reach those places, we require more inner healing.

We find ourselves in crisis, inner crisis, and we think we are a big mistake. We think we are not good enough. Our shadows creep in. We throw in the towel. We give up on ourselves. We beat ourselves up or, if we cannot, we find someone else to beat us up.

How can we so easily forget the places of love we have been in by walking this path? How easily we forget the connections we have made with people, with places, to nature, and to Spirit.

One of humanity's greatest diseases is the disease of forgetfulness. We've forgotten why we came here to this beautiful earth. We've forgotten how much our Earth Mother loves us. We've forgotten our life purpose, and we've forgotten our ancestors' stories. In forgetting so much about our history, where we come from, we began to lose the essence of our souls. We walk a bit like zombies, controlled by something outside ourselves. We end up so disempowered that we begin to blame others. We blame our parents, we blame our partners, we blame the government, and we blame our neighbours, and when we run out of people to blame, we blame ourselves.

So what do we need to reclaim our power, our inner power, and begin to walk again with head up and chest out, tall and strong, proud of who we are and what we achieve day after day? We need to deconstruct the self and unlearn all that we have learnt before. We need to begin with self-love and self-acceptance. We need to go back to our hearts every minute we can. Living from a good place within the heart is essential if we want to teach our children healthy ways. If we want to create a society that is healthy, loving, and connected, we need to go back to our hearts.

The heart is the centre of our being. If we keep forgetting that place, the place of the heart, we risk dying of heart disease or heart failure. We need to keep practising, again and again, to take a deep breath and to enter the heart place. We must not fear entering the heart. Humans have made the greatest creations when using all their faculties together in balance and harmony.

The longest journey I have ever taken in my life was the journey from my head to my heart. The reasons for this are many. Everything taught to me in my society pointed me to be always in my head. And so it is with every mainstream education system in our society.

We need a revolution to take place in our society. If we could start with education, we would be doing our children and grandchildren a great service. We need to teach our children to think with their hearts, to act from their hearts, and to love one another again.

We must not blame the male-dominant system. We are part of that system, having created it ourselves, so we have no call to blame others for it. We have to take responsibility for our reality because we are the ones who create it ourselves.

What can we do? What can we do to change all of what we see outside ourselves, all that we don't like, and all that we see is no longer working? The only way is to change ourselves, our very own selves. How? By going within and deconstructing the self, and by unlearning what we have learnt. By forging new paths to ourselves, we forge new paths to others. Let us start by doing things differently from our norm, by allowing ourselves to think outside the box. As we begin to see and create a new paradigm, we begin to breathe again and rebirth ourselves daily.

We are all great people, unique in our own ways, unique in our feelings. We are tremendously blessed—blessed beyond belief! We need to begin to see our blessings and count them daily. Only then will we begin to live a fulfilled life, a life filled with blessings, because our lives truly will be full of blessings.

Working Shamanically with Young People

I am very passionate about working shamanically with young people.

Young people are highly responsive to shamanic work. They do not have the same barriers and complexity that adults have. They are open. When a shaman-healer connects a young person with his or her guide, he or she is fully connected and supported for life. The young person may stray from the path, but he or she will always know what he or she needs to do, namely go within, ask whatever he or she needs to know, and receive guidance.

My heart sings when a young person comes for shamanic work and goes home fully empowered, fully connected. I have done all kinds of shamanic work with very young people: past life, soul retrieval, power retrieval, clearing or cutting the cords, etc.

After the age of twelve, or for a girl, after she has had her first moon, you can do very much the same work you do with adults for empowerment, taking them into journeys to connect with their inner guides. Young people are very present and much more connected to Spirit than adults are.

With young children under twelve years, the work is a little different. They need to be held more, energetically speaking, and we need to journey for them.

I always recommend for my students to make sessions accessible for children by not charging the parents so there is no financial pressure. Instead, parents can give a donation, something they can afford. I received guidance in a vision quest back in 2004 to work with children. It has been this way since then.

More often than not, the parents themselves have had sessions before, so they have seen how much the shamanic work has helped them. So when they feel that their children are struggling, they ask for sessions for their children too.

I have also worked with my own children since they were very young and they were my teachers in that way. Now young adults, they come for sessions or a cleansing when they feel they need it. At moments such as this, I am not Mum; at that moment, I am the practitioner, I am spirit. The difference is noticeable, even for them, because I always wear my spiritual clothes and beads when I work and the energy and the message is clear: *Right now, I am not Mum.*

It is always a great delight to work with children and young people. The work is not always easy. Sometimes the child carries in his or her aura so much trouble and so much trauma that the session can end up being quite difficult.

Sometimes children come with attachments too. This is more common than we think.

Once upon a time, I was seeing a baby boy of only six months old. He had a terrible energy attached to him. Imagine an octopus engulfing you, strangling you. Such an "octopus" is what this child had around him. The mother had brought him to me because he would burst into screams as if he were in some kind of terrible pain. This would happen almost every day. The first thing I asked was if she had taken him to the doctor. "Yes," she said. "They have done all kinds of tests and exams and have found nothing wrong with him."

When such is the situation, when a doctor cannot find anything wrong with the person, then it is an energy problem, no doubt. When that is the case, an energy worker/shaman-healer might be able to solve the mystery and help.

What I did first was to close my eyes, in order to see with my spiritual eyes. Then I could see the octopus strangling the baby.

I called my spirit animals and guides to help me remove the creature, which was definitely not from this realm.

After the session and after a few weeks had passed, the mother contacted me to say how grateful she was. The boy had been sleeping well since the session and had not had another outburst of crying and screaming since. For some people, this might look and sound like a miracle, but it is not. It is simple: just an average, everyday shamanic work, very normal and very common—at least to me.

When we are aware of energies like those mentioned, we are in an empowered place and can do something about it.

The first time I worked with a child was in 2003. It was a one-month-old baby. As I held his little body, I looked at him and I said to Spirit, "I

am a warrior. Why do you bring a child to me? I cannot heal a child."
Many years have passed since then. I have changed. The feminine power
of the Goddess has entered my heart, and ever since, she has been slowly
opening me up, removing the armour around my heart and healing me,
revealing also the compassionate healer inside.

A year after the encounter with that one-month-old baby, I went on a
vision quest that opened my heart and brought children into my healing
work. In that vision quest, I had a dream of a child about two years old
who had been raped and, as a consequence, had died. The house had been
cordoned off, isolated by the red tape that the police use at a crime scene. I
woke up, startled by that dream. My heart was pounding; I was sweating
and in terror; and I vomited a black bile for what felt like hours.

I was only on the second night of my vision quest and I thought I would
die, but that is how Spirit works. Sometimes we need to be cracked right open.
Traumas from our past lives or our present need to be healed and released for
the light to come in. In the middle of a vision quest, you are alone at night-
time. It is pitch-dark out there. You cannot go anywhere, but you must face
what you need to face. In the darkness of the night, the subconscious is at
work, which is why most of a person's crises happen at night.

That night I prayed very hard for help. I asked all loving spirits to
take that terror away from me. When I stopped vomiting eventually, I fell
asleep. The next day when I awoke, I felt completely clear.

I then carried out my first work helping children at the end of 2004,
by helping raise funds for children in Cape Town, South Africa, where a
friend was working with children affected by or infected with HIV there.
After that work, I did more of the same, helping another friend in Paraiba,
Brazil, who was also working with children affected by HIV, poverty, and/
or physical disability. Then there was the work with Youth Vision, helping
young people at risk of being excluded from school in Edinburgh. Often,
the traumas young people carry are such that they need to be held for a
long period to heal and to get their confidence build up, to become healthy

adults. At the Planetary Healing Centre, Edinburgh, we also offered a holistic well-being project for children for years.

It is only now, years later, writing this book, that I am beginning to realise that during that vision quest all those years ago, the awful dream I had released a past life trauma from my etheric body. Releasing the energy from that past life trauma made me ready for the next phase of my work in this earthly realm.

Animals, like children, also respond well to shamanic work. The same is true for plants, trees, streams, rivers, and even oceans. Of course, we will need a bit more energy than just the energy of one person alone when we work with the ocean. If we remember that every single drop of water in the ocean counts, we will know that any healing we do, be it by one person or a collective, will count. If we can get a collective of people working together, we can accomplish miracles!

Ancestral Healing

Within shamanism, we can go back into the ancestral line and heal ourselves and our ancestors. And when we are working on the vertical axis of above and below, related to past and future, masculine and feminine energies respectively, we benefit in the present by the blessings that are released onto our family members and children.

In the spiritual dimension, time does not exist. Do not perceive life as linear; instead, see it as a circle within a circle within another circle, like a spiral, representing our past and future. The circles encompassing each other represent the many dimensions of ourselves. Anything you change in the past will affect your present and will affect your future.

Two North American grandmothers, one of them Susan Stanton, who had come to Scotland to carry out beautiful ancestral work, had come to help bring together the thirteen grandmothers of Scotland. The world already had the thirteen original grandmothers, and now it was time to bring together the thirteen grandmothers of each country. I organised and supported a few sessions which were done by the two grandmothers. These took place at the Edinburgh Shamanic Centre.

It was there that a mother, along with her six-month-old son, came to see the grandmothers. Her son was of Afro-Brazilian ancestral lineage. As soon as the grandmothers picked up the child to do the healing, he started to cry a deep cry, sobbing as if he was feeling a deep pain inside. The grandmothers then worked on his aura, changing the imprint of pain, sadness, and sorrow.

It is in our history that when the African people came to Brazil, they suffered and endured a pain that was beyond understanding, a pain that left a profound scar in their minds, on their bodies, and on their souls. Of course, the generations that followed feel that pain too.

The grandmothers were adamant: the suffering the boy was carrying was not his alone. He was carrying the suffering of his ancestors.

How many of us walk around in a state of pain, deep pain, which is not ours but is the pain that we inherited from our ancestral line? *All of us.*

To heal that ancestral pain, we first need to connect with our ancestral roots. To know our past is to know our future. By staying grounded and rooted, we are strong and are able to create our future. I recommend you learn about your ancestors, where they came from, and what physical, mental, and emotional battles they fought. What kind of suffering have they gone through? Go back into the history books or elder family members and find out what happened to your ancestors. Connect with them along your vertical axis. From that place, you can heal the past and strengthen the future.

By seeking out the ancestors, reestablishing a connection with them, we are reestablishing a connection to ourselves.

Sometimes it is a matter of claiming our lineage. Adopted children or those whose ancestors had intermarriages sometimes are left with the feeling that they do not belong anywhere or do not have roots.

For almost all my life, I felt I did not belong anywhere, until one day. On that day, I carried out a profound healing to claim my indigenous ancestry. However, what the spirits told me was that for me to claim my indigenous side, I had to first accept my white ancestry. I had a profound dislike for my white ancestry, and therefore I had a profound dislike of myself.

My great-grandmother, an indigenous woman, was married to a white man from Portugal. The story in my family is that he lassoed her and brought her home. As he was a Catholic of "great morals", he married her before they bore three children. An abusive man, he used to beat her up constantly with his horse crop. The worst part about it was that my great-grandmother was not allowed to practise her indigenous spirituality. She was now married to a white man, a Catholic man and, therefore, it was inappropriate to talk about spirits or work with spirits, including doing ceremonies or any form of healing for people.

When I was thirty-three years old, I had a profound spiritual experience that shaped my life. I was in a sweat lodge, and my great-grandmother came to me. She summoned me to start doing shamanic work. The call was really strong and powerful. It was not something I could dismiss or ignore. It stayed with me and shaped me into the person I am today. It was through that reconnection to my ancestral roots that I began to feel strong again.

I had just been through a divorce. I was scattered into what felt like a thousand pieces. I was broken: heart, mind, and spirit. It was during that time of despair that I went deeper spiritually and found who I am.

It is always like this: in times of despair, when we feel broken, dead, or shattered into pieces, Spirit finds a way in. The hard times are not always as they appear. And it is always at the hard times that Spirit comes into our lives.

We all need to learn about our ancestors, learn their story, feel their joy, and feel their pain and heal it. By knowing them, who they are, we know who we are. That truly makes us strong because it gives us deep roots.

A Few Thoughts on Deep Listening, Service, and Unconditional Love

To journey through our stuff, we need something called deep listening. We must listen deeply to our feelings, our emotions, our state of being. Deep listening is an awareness of our deep wounds, our sadness and inner sorrows, that we can touch and release. Some people have deep anger and deep hatred; others have deep sadness, deep sorrows. Others have restlessness, deep fears, and deep anxieties. All of this streams in from our inner child. We need to go deep inside to connect with and "rescue" our inner child and see what is hurting, what we are longing for, what we are attached to, and what does not serve us.

In walking the path of the awakened, we need to be constantly looking within. By making space inside, by releasing the old that no longer serves, we make space for more love—more love for the self. And the more we grow to love and cherish the self, the more we grow to love and cherish others. I am not talking about selfish love; I am talking about deep love and compassion for self and others.

The ocean carries a deep love for you, the earth carries a deep love for you, the air carries a deep love for you, and the fire carries a deep love for you. You must carry a deep love for yourself too, unconditional love, a love that truly cares. When you are able to deeply love yourself, only then are you able to release that love to the universe. Once there, it can become selfless love for others. To serve other beings with compassion, we must serve without expecting anything in return. We must serve without interest. And to serve without interest, we must relinquish all our interests first.

Attend to the self and all your needs, longings, pains, and sorrows. Only then can you truly serve another human being without self-interest or hidden agendas. You need to look within and attend to all your needs. When you relinquish your inner needs, you, as a human being, can serve and love another without any complications, without any sense of duty or burden. Then your serving truly becomes unconditional love.

Listen deep to your own needs, answer all of them, and then begin your daily practice of loving others.

A Few Thoughts on Non-attachment, Generosity, and Love

Non-attachment, generosity, and love are the three qualities I consider essential to have when walking the shaman-healer's path.

A shaman-healer needs to practise non-attachment to material things and to people, including a partner, a spouse, one's children, and one's pets. Practise non-attachment to the titles people give you, good or bad, and non-attachment to any judgements made by you or others.

If you can let go of attachment to property and material things, then you can easily let go of the rest.

With generosity of the spirit, mind, and heart and generosity of words, resources, money, and food, everything around you—including yourself—can feel abundance, can feel cared for and supported.

Generosity in your work, generosity in the light you share, generosity in your ideas and teachings—practise this generosity without expecting anything in return. This is true generosity, a generosity without interest in the outcome, a generosity with your time and the love you give.

Have love for everything. Love everyone equally, having no preferred ones, considering all to be equal in your heart. No one is better or worse, richer or poorer. Love everyone the same. Receive what they give you, whether fifty pence or one hundred pounds, with the same gratitude.

Love heals; love encompasses everything; love illuminates; and love brings peace.

Practise non-attachment, practise generosity, and practise love. These things will bring you closer to the Great Spirit; they will be the ropes you will wear when you leave this earthly realm.

Love and generosity will be the things you will be able to take with you into the afterlife, and the practice of non-attachment is what will set you free.

CHAPTER 4

Shamanism and Self-Care

To reach an inner state of well-being, deep love, and compassion—to reach the state of divinity within—we need to be in constant dialogue with the Divine, both *the divine within and the Divine without.* We require an inner peace to move from ordinary day-to-day life, from an ordinary state of mind, and to release ourselves from that state and seek the divine self within.

It is not through the mind, but it is through the heart that we can reach that state, the state of grace.

As a shaman-healer or a holistic practitioner of any modality, one needs to take good care of the self. Self-care is paramount to one who is walking the path of the healer.

When we work with the pain and traumas of others, including the souls that we help, we do end up with energies trapped in our bodies. As healers, we all have some level of empathy, which means we have a great gift, the ability to feel what other people feel. This gift is useful on many levels when we consciously put it towards being of service to another. When we move to that level of awareness on our spiritual path, we have to release this great burden. We are no longer "victims" of our empathic state; we are in control of that gift, and we can use it more consciously and powerfully to help another. We truly become healers with the ability to remove the pain that people have had trapped in their bodies for years or, in some cases, all their lives. We can shift and move energies at will.

I have a suggestion for anyone struggling with empathic and sensitive feelings—feeling mass consciousness. You yourself will know if you struggle. You usually are unable to enter an environment without feeling other people's pain. If this is you, hang in there. Don't give up. Consciously shift yourself from the place where you are tossed about by the energies to a place where you feel empowered and in control of what is going on. Shift to a state that, when you enter any space, you hold a state of consciousness of being one with everything, one where when you enter the space, you already know you are happy to serve, willing to serve, willing to give, willing to love, and willing to heal.

Yes, there is a big shift in consciousness, one that brings a greater state of being, well-being for the self, and well-being for others. When this shift happens, it is as if a light bulb goes on in a dark room.

Another thing that is important for shaman-healers to do from time to time is to have extraction work done on themselves.

Once, I had seven extractions done. One may wonder, *How can that be possible? Is your energy not clean? Or do you pick up stuff from doing healing work?*

Sometimes we are so busy running around doing this, doing that, that our energy levels go down. Tiredness and stress is a leading cause of disease; therefore, making sure you always take time to rest and replenish is important. When you are a healer, it is very difficult for you to do deep work on yourself. You need someone with higher energy or at least the same energy you have to work on you.

Since we opened the Edinburgh Shamanic Centre in 2003, and then the Planetary Healing Centre, after having a few energetic burnouts, Mark and I began to take time to go away and replenish. We had to be truly resting, doing absolutely nothing. We went on holidays to just eat, sleep, and lie under the sun. For the first fifteen years when we were running both centres, Mark was also a high school teacher, a job he held for seventeen years, with students ranging in age from twelve to eighteen. I always admired him for his bravery and strength being a healer, a shamanic teacher, and a high school teacher. For us, it became necessary that for at least ten weeks a year we take a rest. However, for that we had to go away; otherwise, rest would not happen. Nowadays we take three months of rest a year. I guess that is because the work is much deeper and we are getting older.

Quite a few years back, Mark decided to stop being a high school teacher. It was a pity for the young people because they truly loved him as a teacher. I have never seen someone more loving and giving than Mark. However, I feared that had he not taken that step, he would be compromising his health.

Often on the shamanic path we are asked to let go of things that no longer serve us. Some things are not easy to give up, and neither the mind nor the heart can decide. When you are in such a situation, ask your body to decide, because your body knows.

I always say to my shamanic students, "When you are not able to follow your heart and your mind cannot make a decision, ask your body. Your body always knows."

Also, if you are walking the path of the shaman-healer, it is as important to look after your body as it is to look after your spirit. Yoga, tai chi, meditation, good healthy food, no alcohol, no toxins, and no drugs in the body are all fundamental if you are walking the path of the healer.

Equally important is to have no toxins of the mind, that is no negative thoughts, no putting yourself down, no listening to your inner critic. These are very basic shamanic inner practices.

Caveman, Cavewoman, Stone People

On one of our holidays, in Greece, I found many amazing caves to sit and relax. The peacefulness of a cave is akin to that of the womb. That is probably what yogis and sages have found in caves. Your thoughts are contained; your energy field is contained and held by the stones around you. Your filaments cannot engage with anyone or anything, so you cannot be distracted or entangled with the filaments of other things or people.

The stones in a cave have a particular form of energy which does not tangle with ours. That is because they have no needs or agendas; they have mastered themselves and their needs over time by being in peaceful meditation. Therefore, they sit there without disturbing our energy. All they do is hold us as the wall of the womb does, holding us in love and peace, nurturing the child within, and bringing peace and nurturing feelings.

Caves are also good at showing us the fear we hold inside ourselves, especially dark caves. Inside a cave, there is nowhere to go, nowhere to hide. If the fears inside us have nowhere to go, they bounce off the walls of the cave. We can run from them, or else we have to face them with ruthless compassion and kill them—or embrace them, and transmute and transform them.

Stones are fascinating beings. Old and wise, they have mastered needs, greed, and emotions. With time they become solid, their knowledge fossilised inside them. They do not reveal what they know to just anyone. They do not waste their time with those who are not ready for their peal of wisdom. They choose carefully whom they reveal their secrets, their knowledge, and their wisdom to. For you to be worthy of their trust and knowledge, you need to have a heart like a child, open, pure, and nonjudgemental.

Even still, when you have all those things, the spirits will take time to impart to you what they know.

When Mark and I began to work with the Stone People, they did not reveal much to us. They waited to see how pure of heart we were. They waited to see what we were doing with the knowledge they were revealing to us bit by bit and how much we were working on ourselves to clear our blockages and limitations. The spirits need to know we are all doing that. After fifteen years of offering Feather Stone Energy Healing training, still to this day the stones are only just beginning to reveal themselves to us.

If you have a stone as a friend, it will be your friends forever. Their lifespan is, of course, much longer than ours is. When we were born, they had already been here for a very long time. When we die and our grandchildren die, they will still be here.

Owing to the type of energy they hold, as in what they have mastered themselves, the stones have mastered neediness. Their medicine is pure and strong. They also carry the medicine of protection, and they will defend you if needed. I remember throwing stones at boys who wanted to fight me and my girlfriends when I was a child. Because of my many traumas, I have almost no memories from my childhood, but I will never forget that one. It was because of the stones that the boys left us alone, unable to get to us.

I have always wondered if the stones are masculine or feminine in gender, so one time I asked them. They told me that like grandfather tobacco, they hold both energies well balanced within themselves. We can choose what to call them, *grandfather stone* or *grandmother stone.*

Fear has power to it, a power that can either kill us or transform us. Either way, the battle with the spirit of fear can leave a big scar in the psyche and in the psyches of many lives to come.

I have worked on many fears on myself, the greatest one being the fear of being seen. I do not yet know exactly where this fear comes from. Is it from my indigenous ancestors, the fear of being seen and decimated; or is it from my childhood, the fear of being seen by my mentally ill mother; or did it come from past lives, being a healer and burned at the stake because of my gifts? I guess it would be truthful to say that it is all of the above.

I usually say that the reason why I am living in Scotland is that I came here to complete my work. Scotland has burned more witches than has any other country in the world. Therefore, it is this place which I have come home to, back home, to complete my work.

Energy Healing

How I wish that all the people of this earth could see energy, touch it, move it, and understand it. Our world would probably be evermore disease-free if such were the case. Many of the problems people experience as diseases are, in fact, energies out of place—energy misplaced and out of balance in the body.

The Chinese people are quite advanced in regards to understanding energies, with acupuncture and herbalism being used to resolve energy imbalances and most problems in the body.

India is also quite advanced with yoga and Ayurveda, traditions that are thousands of years old that address the imbalance of energy and problems in the body.

Shamanism sees the same, namely energy in the wrong place. Energy blockages can cause an infinite number of problems for people. If only we all could see that and treat ourselves spiritually, energetically, not only physically, then our well-being would improve dramatically.

We are all too addicted to the pills to remedy this and to remedy that, seeking a quick fix that can cause us long-term problems. We have forgotten the traditional, natural ways of our ancestors, dismissing them as old folklore.

We need to remember that our human body has a natural way of healing itself. Keeping our energy balanced is all we need to do.

In shamanism, we can go beyond blockages in the physical body caused by problems in this life to work on the blockages of energy that happened in another life. We are all energy. When we die, our consciousness returns to Source, and depending if there are still lessons we need to continue learning, we return by reincarnating again. However, if we have had traumas from other lives, we still bring those memories with us into our blueprint, into our unconscious, where they sit as residue of other past lives.

The more we evolve spiritually, the more we can access past life memories. These memories may be good or may be traumatic. Usually, they are a combination of both. For example, I know how to do certain types of healing work without having an external teacher who taught me. I have this knowledge because my soul remembers. Equally, the deeper I go spiritually, the more my soul begins to remember the traumas I had from past lives. For example, I lived a life as a young girl captured in Africa and taken to the Americas to be a slave. A metal collar was put around my neck, and I had to live with it the rest of that life. I died by being strangled by that collar. The imprint this left on my ethereal body has affected me in so many ways in this life.

For many years I wanted to write this book, but I had no confidence, courage, inspiration, or time. I then began to do a lot of inner work on myself, releasing many things that were preventing my soul from shining or preventing me from writing the book. Contrary to my belief, my problems were, in this life, mostly rooted in my past lives, some are also from my ancestors' line.

My subconscious would always play the message, *I am not good enough. It is not possible. Who am I to write a book?* and so on.

The more we evolve spiritually on the shamanic path, the more we clear stuff and the more we can access past life memories. Sometimes those memories are good, and sometimes they are not. We must work with what we are given at the time.

As we clear and clear, new layers begin to present themselves. So we ask: "What is the purpose of clearing so much stuff? What is the purpose of clearing our Earth Mother of rubbish?" Why do we pick up rubbish from nature when we go for our walks? We do it simply because all that rubbish clogs Mother Earth. It clogs our oceans, clogs the insides of the fishes, and causes damage, pollution, toxic messes, and air toxins in the long term.

A similar thing can be said of our past traumas: we remove energy blockages from our bodies, our minds, our hearts, and our spirits so our energy can flow.

There is a complication, however, which is that the more we clear, the more there is to clear. However, once we remove an energetic blockage, we allow more life force to come in. More health, more inspiration, more life, and more joy can also come in. That is the reason why we remove energetic blockages, so that more life force can flow.

The things I am saying here are not easy to believe by just reading them somewhere in a book. These things need to be experienced for one to believe, for one to truly know.

We are like onions; there are layers and layers of stuff inside us. Deep inside us, there is a sweetness, a kindness, a compassion, and divine being, all covered up by layers and layers of trauma that we experience in human life after human life. Our birth is the first trauma we experience, then life carries on. As it is a very normal life, we experience more traumas. These traumas cause us to accumulate a lot of suffering, and because of this we gain another "ring" around ourselves to protect our sweetness, our love, our heart, our pure essence.

With the many layers we accumulate, we often end up not knowing who we are, what makes our hearts sing, or what brings us joy. We don't even know how to discern the truth from non-truth any more.

Well, let us not paint such a gloomy picture of life, because life is not always just that. Life has its beauty. Let us remember to count our blessings, the innumerable moments we have of connection, of love, and of the friendship that life presents us with. We should not always focus on the bad things, as life is full of mysteries and great joy.

The world would be much better if we would all live as much happier and healthier beings. We would all see, believe, and work with energies. Of that I have no doubt.

New Levels of Working with Energies

What is it that we need to learn about reaching a new level of working with energies?

Firstly, we need to learn to be comfortable, always very comfortable. This is very important. To be able to work at this level, we cannot afford to be concerned with the physical world or bodily processes such as being cold, hungry, or tired.

We need to feel safe, we need to be relaxed, and we need to be able to disconnect from the physical world. This will bring us to another level of awareness. What we will be doing at this next level of awareness is channelling what we have learnt from the spirit world into the physical world.

If we are carrying out a healing, we are bringing through the energy that we can "put our hands on" in the spiritual world and taking it into the physical level of the person receiving the healing. However, there is a much deeper level for us to move to, and for this, awareness of the physical world has to be removed completely. For one to have the ability to work in this way, one must still learn a few things and have a few edges smoothed out. This is what will prepare a person for this other level.

This other level feels very much connected to the head. Indeed, it is this phenomenon of the physical world, our intelligence, that we will be working with, which will connect us to our crown chakra. For us to connect to that level, we first need the heart chakra to be open. Although we may feel we are in our heads, we are not. We are working from our hearts. Coming from the heart, we will find that communication is easier. The more we work this way, the easier it will become. Our job is always to come from the heart. Whatever we do, whatever we say, and whatever words come from our mouths should come from a place of love and divine beauty.

The teachings on this level are very much concerned with other people, with how we can move forward with another step in consciousness to support our fellow beings. It is the direction of north on the medicine wheel where we no longer need to be concerned with the self, for here the self is at peace. However, the self needs to learn to be at peace with others too. If there is still conflict with others, those little sharp edges of the self will need to be smoothed or removed. This will bring us to a place of communion with others and all that is. At this level of consciousness of joy and beauty, our heads are going to be of great help to us. However, we do have to watch out for the traps set by the mind.

For us to be fully learning the lessons of this level, we must always bring ourselves back to the heart. The last attainment is the heart connection, which is only achieved when the heart is fully developed and open. Are you ready to move to this deeper level?

We need to be constantly aware and conscious all the time, for fear will make itself known. The way to deal with fear is very gently, to give it healing, to calm it down. Do not allow the mind to take over. The crucial balance lies between the heart and the mind.

This level of attainment is one of the hardest. We have now found the path of the heart, but the path of the heart is still new to us. Therefore, we will always need to keep checking, asking ourselves, *When I walk this new path, does it feel soft under my feet?* If the path does not feel soft under your feet, then you are on the wrong track. All our life we may have been walking the wrong track. In contrast, the path of the heart is smooth, not hard at all. It is the most beautiful and easiest path to walk.

Wanting to know why is natural. Wanting to understand is natural. After all, understanding is food for the mind. However, always remember that you do not have to understand fully. You do not have to comprehend. All you have to do is trust in the process of here and now. The process knows better. The process has its maturity, its wisdom. You may not understand right away, but all will become clear in time.

In this new level of attainment, we do not concern ourselves with explanations, with understanding the mechanics of this or that, or with what is supposed to be best or worst. We must only concern ourselves with the highest purpose, aligning ourselves with the highest truth, the highest understanding, and the greatest compassion. For it is from this place that we can, and shall, work. We must not be concerned with matters of the physical world, for the spirits will take care of those. They might be slow, and they might take some time, but they will assist. They will be able to resolve the concerns we have in the physical world; we just need to hand those problems over to Spirit.

Our job is to stand and open our hands in prayer. Be open, humble, and joyful. Yes, fear will always crop up, but we must not allow that to deter us. Let Spirit help us; let Spirit show us what to do. Trust in the wisdom of the higher self, the higher the state of being, the greater light.

We are moving towards a new era, a new time of great consciousness, and the struggle is greatest for those who are unable to let go, to stop making judgements, or to see beyond the physical world of the self. Yet with time, guided through the struggle, we shall move to a new level of consciousness, a higher and more expansive level. In this task, we must all move forward together. The more we open ourselves up and move to this new level, the more we will be helping others who are struggling to do the same, to move beyond the apparent duality of the two worlds and to come to the place where all is one.

Sharing our thoughts, our heart, our joy, and our wisdom with others: this is who we truly are. And we achieve new spiritual levels when we relinquish the self.

Ceremonies and Rituals

Unfortunately, modern society has lost contact with the sacred; our lives are full of meaningless activities that might fulfil our minds, but not our spirits or our souls.

However, until we are ready, until we are mature enough spiritually, until we complete the cycle of the physical realm, the spiritual realm will not reveal itself to us. The light bulb will not turn on until there is a need for it.

Often the spiritual awakening comes accompanied by life crises. It is not always easy for us to see this because suffering clouds our vision.

Pain, disillusionment, and feelings of giving up are all part of a spiritual awakening. The crises we are experiencing in life in the physical realm are a reflection of how our souls are feeling. Usually, a midlife crisis is a result of spiritual awakening. It's like a crack needing to open up in the psyche so that one may give birth to one's soul. Spiritual rebirths are always accompanied by some form of pain because the rebirth requires expansion in one way or another.

Our mothers gave birth to our physical selves; now we need to give birth to our spiritual selves, ourselves. Life on earth is a cycle of birth, rebirths, and deaths.

There is a way to make the rebirth process less painful, less crisis-like, and that is by doing ceremonies, consciously marking every "contraction" we feel with some meaningful work with some meaningful sacred time and action.

Acknowledging the parts of us that are dying in the process is important. Acknowledging all that we are is important. Doing this consciously brings a sense of control and a sense of peace to any process and any life crisis we experience. Finding the sacred and bringing it back to our lives is akin to finding an experienced doctor or midwife to support our re-birth.

Ceremonies accompany human beings all our lives. Humans have attempted to create ceremonies since the very beginning of time because some part of us knows that the sacred is who we are. The sacred is the food that feeds and nurtures our souls. Without the sacred in our lives, we will perish and disappear from the face of the earth. Without the sacred, we create wars to kill one another. Without the sacred, we cannot recognise the sacred in another.

For the sake of ourselves and for the sake of our children and grandchildren, we need to find the sacred again and reinstate it in our lives.

So why am I talking about ceremony and not rituals? Rituals are another sacred way of creating the sacred, but a ritual requires a lot more time and mind, as it has to be performed as a repeating set of procedures.

The procedure has to be followed always in the same way, using the exact same words, if it is to work. The process for this is akin to following a recipe: it is very specific.

For example, the Catholic Church has a ritual of transubstantiation. The ritual is performed exactly the same all over the world in a specific way. It is not possible to change it; there is no room for making it in a different way. One will recognise this ritual of the Catholic Church anywhere in the world. No matter where one is or what language is spoken, the ritual is always the same.

With ceremonies, it is different. There is a sacredness to a ceremony, but equally, there is room for inspiration to come, so a ceremony is performed slightly differently from a ritual depending on where you are in the world, depending on the culture, and depending on what is available at the time. Ceremonies are by nature a little more flexible, allowing creativity to come in, allowing space to breathe, and allowing the heart to enter into the picture. With a ceremony, the one performing it doesn't have to remember everything and doesn't have to follow precise instructions. The shaman-healer performing a ceremony is allowed to have Spirit come in and bring a new order to things, new words, and new ways, all according to the energy that is there.

Perhaps because I have a terrible memory, ceremony has revealed itself to me, and I have fallen in love with it since then.

So we ask, what was performed by our ancestors, ceremony or rituals? The answer is both. There are times when rituals are called for, and there are times when ceremonies are called for. One needs to identify what one is doing and decide what comes easier and what is appropriate for the occasion.

In shamanism there is no right or wrong, no better or worse; it just is. As long as your heart is pure and your intention is pure, the way you do things becomes pure too.

In Alignment with Truth

How can we keep ourselves in alignment with truth all the time? And how do we get our energy tangled?

When in our hearts we feel one thing and either don't say it or don't act on it immediately, we will encounter a problem down the line, 100 per cent guaranteed.

Usually it is not easy for people to identify the truth within themselves. This is because we all need to have full confidence in ourselves, in our judgement, and in our discernment. That in itself can be a lifelong journey to achieve, but when we begin to trust our feelings about things and people, that journey is half over.

This brings us back to the alignment of heart, mind, and spirit I spoke of before. For us to be able to make good judgements and trust our intuition, we need to learn to use all our faculties: heart, mind, and spirit.

Always be truthful about everything. That way you'll always keep your energy clear. There will be almost no misunderstanding happening around you. There will be no leaking of energy or draining of energy, just clear communication, clear connection, and transparency.

Of course, if you are a person who is truthful about everything, you will encounter other people who are like that, and they will align energetically with you. And then there will be the people who are not like that and who will have problems with you and your ways. About those, I would just say to let them go.

Some people say that with me, they know where they are. However, I haven't learnt to give off such an impression overnight, and I was not born with this quality. On the contrary, I had to work all my life—and I still have to constantly work on this.

I first thought that I was rude. Then I thought my way of communicating was foreign and that I needed to learn the British way, which is more polite. However, with time I realised my problem had nothing to do with culture, language, or politeness, although consciously adding a bit of politeness to my way of communicating did make a difference. No, I found out it had more to do with energy than anything else, namely the energy that lets one know when something rings true and when it doesn't.

It is not easy when you read energies, because you are usually not listening to what the person is saying. Instead, you are listening to the energy behind what the person is saying.

We all have the capacity to read energies. My children can do it too. It is not something I taught them; they just have it. They used to read their teachers at high school and knew when the teachers were in alignment with the truth and when they were not. Now my children use this skill all the time.

Just like we all have intuition, I believe everyone also has the capacity to read energies. If we don't focus on the words but focus on how we feel when the person says something, then we will be practising reading energy.

Practising reading energy and practising aligning ourselves with truth all the time will save us a lot of energetic entanglements in life.

Equally, we need to be ready to hear the truth without fear. That will save us a lot of headaches and heartbreaks. We need to give full permission to the people around us to be truthful. When we do that, we are creating not only a new culture around us but also a new consciousness, one based on truth and aligned with truth.

And then there are the times when we do things or say things because we are feeling sorry for the person we are trying to help. This is not aligned with the truth. We are seeing the person in a place of disempowerment, and instead of taking them out of that place of victim, our actions or words are keeping them in there. How many times have I done that!

We need to do things because they feel good and feel right and because they are aligned with the truth. Seeing a person as a victim is to be unaligned with the highest truth.

This is not an easy practice. Sometimes I make decisions, say things, or take actions which, only a few days or sometimes weeks later, I realise are not aligned with the highest truth. When that happens, I refrain from giving myself a hard time, as to do so would be a waste of my good energy, and instead I just change and align with the highest truth right there and then. Energy and power begin to return to me at that moment.

The Mystery of Life

From the moment we are born, we enter the mystery of life as little children, little babies.

As we grow up, life tosses us around. Sometimes we hang onto our lives by just a little thread and we try to understand the mystery of life by walking a spiritual path. We then begin to encounter more peaceful mornings in our life. We also begin to notice the sunset.

One thing is true: there is no better place or more beautiful place than earth, our Mother. The beauty is why so many souls choose to come here and experience life in this earthly realm.

All places, all directions, on the earth are stunning. They each hold unique vibrations and have so much to offer us for exploration and learning.

If only we could see things from the perspective of the spirits, who haven't got a body to inhabit and who are themselves free and liberated, free to move and go about. Some spirits choose to no longer incarnate. They forsake the pleasures of the body and the pain of the body to be free, to be just pure consciousness moving around. They are consciousness that interacts with humans, between worlds, but they are so evolved that they no longer need physical bodies.

These spirits inhabit sacred caves, sacred lands, ley lines, sacred wells, and Neolithic structures. They inhabit portals created by humans, portals created by spirits, and places in nature. They have no agenda of their own; they are free from ego and mind. They cast no shadow. Humans who are ready to enter silence become aware of them. Where these spirits are called to help, they go. Where help is needed, they go. They arrive unassumingly; they arrive free. On their pilgrimage through the earth, they sometimes stop in caves, sacred openings, and rest there for a while. They greet the humans who arrive who are quiet enough to sense them.

These spirits tune into your vibration, the vibration of your heart. They feel you, they sense you, and they read you. They don't reveal themselves to many, because many are not ready. Even when they reveal themselves, sometimes even those who are ready still don't take time to listen, take time to sense, or take time to sit in pure stillness.

It is in the stillness of the mind and the stillness of the body that our spirit can communicate with these other spirits. It is in the centre of the self that all begins, as the centre is the place of Spirit, the creativity of Spirit, and the generosity of Spirit. This is a place that is nonjudgemental, not critical of self or others.

That is where Spirit resides. That is where Spirit fills us up with knowledge, wisdom, abundance, and love. Not with material things, because material things do not concern Spirit. The Spirit fills us up with deep knowing, deep wisdom, deep clarity, and deep peace.

That is why sages seek caves. It is also why shaman-healers live on the edge of the community and never within the hustle and bustle. They live amidst the peace in the mountains, amidst the peace in nature, so they can hear spirits and interact with them. For it is in the quietness of the cave, the quietness of nature, that the spirits live.

If you want to connect with the shaman-healer in yourself, seek quietness. Seek the cave inside yourself. Enter it in silence and reverence. Enter it to enrich your life and to commune with the spirits. Enter without expectations. Enter with an open heart. Enter to connect with the spirit world and disconnect from the physical world.

It is necessary to disengage and is necessary to leave people behind, because the place you are entering is a sacred cave hidden within. Always going within is how we will find the answers. Always within is where we will find our strength. The love we seek to feel for humanity is also there. The voice of the ancestors is also there.

The voice of the ancestors comes to us on the whispering of the wind. The ancestors whisper what they want to reveal to us: things about the origins of time, the origins of life, our lives in this earthly realm, and the gracefulness we carry in ourselves. They whisper to us of the beauty and power of the sea goddess, of her soothing sounds, of her all-giving attitude towards life.

We need to listen to the sounds of the ancestors and the spirits of the land. They are all different wherever we go. They speak with a different sound. They give a unique blessing.

When we are tired or old and the time comes for us to release our body, our sacred rope, either the land or the fire will take our rope. They will dispose of it for us. We will be honoured, and with time we will each become an ancestor. We will give of our blessing and of our love to the ones left behind, the ones who were not yet ready to accompany us to the other realm, the realm of spirit.

Our generosity of spirit, the love we gave and created around us, is what we will take with us. This will be the rope we will wear in the other life. The forgiveness we gave to ourselves and to others will be the key that will open the doors of the other realms, into which we will enter quietly and proud.

CHAPTER 5

The Return of the Divine Feminine

Amongst many goddesses in my heart, there are three goddesses who have a special place in my heart, my mind, and sometimes my body: the sea goddess Yemanjá, the goddess Kwan-Yin and Mary Magdalene. They teach love and compassion for humanity.

When the divine feminine returns to her place of empowerment, human beings will find peace within their hearts, their minds, and their bodies.

The goddesses speak of life, giving life and sustaining life on our planet Earth. As humanity begins to align more with the giving and sustaining of life, sustainability will become number one on our agenda.

As humanity aligns itself more with compassion, suffering will begin to disappear and equality will be given a place in our agenda.

The deep love of the Goddess that flows to and through each one of us brings peace to this earthly realm.

More work nurturing the divine feminine within each one of us human beings is needed on the earth. Where the feminine is empowered, children, elders, and men are empowered.

More work to bring the divine feminine and divine masculine into full empowerment and balance is required to bring more balance to our earthly realm.

The Mother gives life and love. The feminine nurtures and supports life, bringing compassion and love to all human beings.

Having our centre so close to the sea, has allowed me to feel the power of the sea goddess over the years. It has allowed me to build a relationship with her and to see her at work on many occasions, clearing, cleansing, and purifying our centre. I don't know how we would've managed without her cleansing and purification. The centre used to have sixteen volunteer therapists working alternating in there, so the amount of energy transmuted on a daily basis by the sea goddess is not possible to describe.

All the volunteers who work at the Planetary Healing Centre or who have worked there before come, or came, because they hold unconditional love and compassion in their hearts. Like Kwan-Yin, they hear the cries of humanity. They bring the balm of healing to each and every person they see in the holistic project, soothing their pain. They work relentlessly with very little rest to heal those who are afflicted by pain, broken, and fragmented while walking their human path on this earth.

Each volunteer is a drop in the ocean of love, in the ocean of compassion, helping to form and shape the ocean of the divine feminine, which is one of love and compassion.

Each volunteer gives of his or her time without expecting anything in return. Some have been there volunteering for fifteen years, some for ten years, and others for eight years. Some come and go; others stay. All of them work tirelessly, giving tirelessly so that those suffering feel the gentleness of the Goddess touching their faces and drying their tears. The volunteers are there so that those in pain may receive and release, so that those grieving can release their sadness and sorrows into the heart and hand of the Goddess. She expresses herself through men and women therapist volunteers. She chooses no gender for she has no gender herself. Kwan-Yin was thought to be a male bodhisattva, then with time she was thought to be female. This was to show that she chooses no gender, has no preferences, and holds both male and female consciousness within herself.

93

The healing balm of the Goddess is felt at the Planetary Healing Centre. Men, women, elders, and children receive the compassion of the Goddess and the love of the Goddess.

Through her love, the Goddess heals. Through her love, she brings peace to the hearts of people, to the lives of people, to the surface of this earth. Through the balm of healing, she brings the love that touches life and brings balance to life once more.

Let's Talk about a Taboo Subject: Abortion

Often women will come to me for healing work because they have gone through an abortion.

To have an abortion is not an easy decision to make. It's also not an easy decision to talk about since the female body was made to create and support life.

Abortion is one of the hardest things for a woman to go through because it involves a lot of things, including feelings, perspectives, morals, and fears; requires agreement or spurs disagreement; makes some people feel guilty; causes some to keep it a secret; and leads a woman sometimes to fear other people's judgements, disapproval, and so on. So for a woman to go through all of that even before she makes a decision is really hard. Often she will find herself disempowered for a long time after an abortion, along with having feelings of guilt and confusion.

I believe souls make their way here and that they choose their parents to learn from. If their parents are not ready for them, they have to go back and either wait until their chosen parents are ready or choose a different set of parents who will give them similar experience and teachings in the earthly realm.

In the process of abortion, women can lose their confidence and their trust in themselves, and it can take a long time for them to retrieve these things. This means a loss of power occurred. Soul loss can also occur in the process of abortion, with happiness and joy leaving. It is also very common for a woman who has had an abortion to lose her sense of direction in life. So soul retrieval to bring back the fragmented self is very important for the healing.

Amidst so much confusion, it sometimes happens that part of the person's soul attaches itself to the soul of the foetus, in an attempt to look after the latter soul in other dimensions.

Sometimes the feeling of guilt and shame is such that a soul part leaves, unable to bear those feelings.

As part of the healing process after an abortion, sometimes women feel the need for a ceremony.

Also, sometimes a woman comes for healing for the abortion, but after talking together, we find that her real problem is something much deeper. But sometimes the opposite is also true: she comes for something else, and we find out that an abortion is the root problem of what she is experiencing right now.

In some countries, abortion is legal; in others, it is illegal. So sometimes women have to also become "outlaws" if they make such a decision. The feeling of devastation can take a long time to heal.

A sacred circle of sisters can be a good place to start the healing. There is nothing more powerful than sitting in a safe sacred circle of women and talking about things that are very deep and dear to us, things that we are not able to talk about in other places or other circles.

The loving acceptance and unconditional love that women bring when sitting together in the sacred circle is phenomenal.

Just being able to talk about an abortion for the first time to other women who you know will not judge you is already a great healing experience or else the first step taken towards the healing. Of course one needs to be ready for healing, as it is not possible to force things when one is not ready.

In all the healings I have done, I have never found the soul of a foetus lost or stuck in between worlds. The spirits have told me that before an infant enters the physical realm through birth, it is more like the essence of angels, and because of this, it knows its way in the spiritual realm and knows the way back home because in its journey to the physical realm, it has not gone far from home. Because a foetus hasn't yet fully entered the physical realm, it is not possible for it to get lost or stuck anywhere.

Some souls are very clear and persistent about the parents or the mother they choose to learn from. Often if these souls are sent back, they will find their way down here again very quickly. Usually within less than three months, the mother will be pregnant again. I have seen a few cases like that. Those kinds of souls usually know who they are, know the lessons they want to learn in the earthly realm, and are very clear from whom they want to learn these lessons from.

Counselling can be a good start for some women, but for those who are ready to go beyond the understanding of the mind and do their healing on a spiritual level, shamanic healing is good.

If you have gone through an abortion and feel you need healing, performing the following very powerful ceremony might help:

Buy some flowers, or pick some flowers from your garden or some wild flowers from out in nature. Find a place in nature where you will not be disturbed by anyone for a while.

Close your eyes and visualise yourself entering the cave of your womb. Go in deeper and deeper. Look for the feminine spirit of your cave, your womb. When you see her, let her know you came for healing. Communicate to her what healing you are seeking. Is it to regain your confidence? release shame? release feelings of guilt? release sadness? Look deep inside of yourself and find out what type of healing you are seeking.

If there are tears that seek to be released, then release them. If there are words to be expressed to the child you did not have, then let the words come. If you feel that you need to ask for forgiveness, then ask for it. Do and say what comes to your heart to do and say. It is your ceremony for healing, and because of this, it is a very powerful one.

If you feel your work is to say goodbye, then say goodbye. If you feel your work is to talk to the child you did not have and explain what happened, including the circumstances of your life at the time of the abortion, then have that talk with the child.

Then forgive yourself. Release yourself from all forms of guilt and sadness.

Bless your womb-cave, bless the essence of the soul, release him or her, and say goodbye. Then fill yourself with gratitude—gratitude to the soul for choosing you, and gratitude to your womb for not holding onto the sadness from this experience.

When all is completed, begin humming, making soothing sounds, chanting or sing a healing song, any song you know and like. Sing for healing yourself. Sing to free your voice again and also to free any shame you have been carrying in your voice arising from this experience. Let the healing enter your voice, your mind, your heart, your womb, and your spirit. Feel gratitude for this healing you have received.

Then visualise yourself coming back from the womb-cave to the place where you are in nature. Visualise your womb healed and cleansed, strong and vibrant again. In your voice, notice that you carry confidence again. In your voice you carry joy once more.

Now take the flowers you brought with you and do an offering. If there is a stream, you can put the flowers one by one into the stream. Watch them float away as you feel the gratitude in your heart. If there is no stream, leave the flowers under a tree or in the earth where you did your ceremony for healing.

Sexual Abuse and Violation

One's relationship with one's body must be a sacred relationship of deep love and respect. The body is the vehicle of the soul and the spirit. We must each see our body as the sanctuary where the Divine resides.

Any act of violation against the body is an act of violation against the Divine.

Building a relationship of closeness to your body by caring for it, providing it with healthy food, and providing it with healthy sexual relationships is very important.

The relationship one have with one's body mirrors how one feels inside. Sacred sexuality, a sexuality that is based in love and respect, must be our aim at all times.

Our sexuality is a doorway to our soul. It is a doorway to the Divinity within us, in the same way that a prayer or a ceremony is a doorway to reach the Divine inside ourselves.

Therefore, our sexual energy must be clean, direct, and purposeful. It must hold within it deep love not only for our partner but also for us.

To see men and women who come for healing work who have had violent acts committed against them in childhood against their will, against their wishes, without their permission, is quite upsetting.

Often the innocent child who has been violated has had his or her soul ripped out of them and is in a place hard to reach. It really saddens me to see how people can be broken and deeply fragmented by such cruel acts of violation against them.

To bring them back home is one of the most beautiful works to do. To bring back the innocent child who has been lost for a very long time, lonely and sad, devastated, and feeling unsafe, is the greatest gift of healing work. There is no description or words to do justice to such a blessing.

Often people who were violated sexually spin into a dark place, a place that only those with absolute deep love can reach.

In order to cope with the trauma, in order to survive it, the essence of the soul splits from the person. It is very common that more than one soul loss occurs. Often, as well as the soul part, the shaman-healer also needs to bring the person's power back. The perpetrator of the crime robs the child of his or her light and sometimes also robs him or her of the will to carry on afterwards. Power, strength, and ruthlessness are all necessary to take back the light that belongs to the child and return the child fully empowered to the adult self.

Sexuality is sacred, so when it becomes an act of violence and terror, it can devastate a person almost beyond repair. However, thanks to soul retrieval work, it is possible to bring back the many fragments of the person.

For people who have had such trauma, six months to a year, or even longer, of shamanic work is recommended, at least once a month, to gradually empower the person, retrieve his or her soul parts, and help him or her to start again.

Often people who have been sexually abused come for shamanic work after they have gone through years of counselling as they still feel the trauma has not been cleared. This is because there is only so much that the human mind can understand and only so much that we can release emotionally through talk therapy. On a spiritual level, the person also needs to be helped because the tear left in his or her psyche can only be mended by bringing back what he or she has lost in the first place.

As for the perpetrator, often he or she has been abused himself or herself. The perpetrator's soul is broken too, fragmented almost beyond repair. It is important to see every human being who comes to you for help when you are a shaman-healer. The work goes beyond the healer's mind, it has to be done with your heart. Perpetrators too seek to heal and mend their broken selves. They too want their souls to come back home.

One requires an infinite amount of love and compassion to walk the shamanic path. Many are called but few answer the call.

The shamanic path is beautiful, filled with deep love and compassion for self and for others. When we let go of our small selves and become our greater selves, everything becomes much easier because the work is done by the spirits; we are the assistants in the physical realm. If we are able to hold no judgements, then we are able to hold deep compassion for humanity, with deep compassion being what humanity needs to heal.

Connecting with Spirit

We are afraid of the unknown; we are afraid to misappropriate; we are afraid to connect. That sense of disconnection and fear goes way back to our ancestors, and if we don't heal it in ourselves, our children will inherit our disconnection too.

How can we free our mind and connect? We can make a start by realising our fears and releasing them one by one. Instead of feeding them and giving them power, we need to heal them and release them. We need to realise where they are coming from and then let them go.

There are also fears that are not ours that we pick up from other people, through their misconception, misunderstandings, anger, ignorance and pain. And what is worse, we take on those fears and make them our own.

Some fears that we have, we don't even know where they come from, but we take them anyway.

We need to stop and take stock of how many fears we have, where they come from, and if they are serving us. We will find that 90 per cent of them do not serve for anything apart from creating anxieties, separation, and confusion.

If we can just accept ourselves and all that the universe gives us on a daily basis, we will be in a much better place within.

Every fear that enters your mind, stop it, pick it up, analyse it, and desecrate it. Look at it and ask yourself: where is this creature who is trying to enter my mind coming from? Look at it and see how it appears: Is it ugly? beautiful? sad? Before you take it in, check if it is worth your time, your energy, your attention, and your power. Don't just take any rubbish in, as sometimes these fears remain for a long time, making themselves comfortable and at home. They end up making a mess of your sacred home. No longer is there silence and stillness once they enter, only their voices constantly nagging at you and eating your energy. Go inside, take stock, make space for inspiration of the highest sort to come to you, make space for peace to come to you, and make space for acts of love to come to you in this earthly realm. Then you will have a life worth living and a mind that is not cluttered. Then peace and silence will enter you. And when peace and silence enter you, all the good people and all the good spirits will want to be around you. They will want to be around you because they want a bit of that peace and silence too. And in that silence they will teach you, inspire you, and guide you.

If you want to paint, the spirits will paint with you. If you want to write, they will write with you. If you want to heal, they will heal with you. All that is needed is for you to stop for a moment and take stock of what it is that you allow to enter your mind and your heart.

You have gateways in you too. Your mind is a gateway, as is your heart, your body, and your spirit. What is it that you allow to come through your gateways? What kind of food do you allow through the gateway of your body? Are you a good guardian of yourself? Or do you let in drinks or drugs that stimulate your mind and rob you of your peace? Do you let in food that clogs your arteries and blocks your heart, or do you allow in food that nurtures you and supports you?

Are you aware? Are you really aware, or are you just pretending to be aware? Are you awake? Are you truly awake, or are you half asleep? You can't make excuses any more.

We humans cocreate with the spirits all the time. The spirits know what they want to create. What about you? Do you know what you want to create? Do you know what you want the spirits to create with you?

Every time you have a thought that is contracting or limiting, release it. Don't feed it, because if you do, you will be feeding limitations in your life. Seek the thoughts that are expansive, the thoughts that are always saying yes to life. Remove from your life the "no" that you always give in reply to the questions asked by the universe.

Create light and expansiveness around you all the time. Don't be afraid, for the universe does not know what is possible and what is not possible. The universe simply picks up on your thoughts and then simply creates what they dictate by expanding and contracting. So if you have a thought that is limiting, the universe picks it up and creates the limitation.

So from today on, imagine that you are at the gatekeeper of your mind and all the thoughts that are limiting you are not being allowed in. Can you imagine the wonderful things you will create by only allowing the positive and expansive thoughts to come in?

Now you are beginning to see the bigger picture.

It is not possible to hear spirits' whispers if your interior is noisy and cluttered. The inspiration cannot come in if one's inside is stimulated by caffeine, processed food, or flashing lights from computer or mobile phone screens. It is not possible for Spirit to enter because there is no space in there. Spirit like quietness, peace, silence, and stillness.

That is why spiritual people go to caves, because it is there they find silence and stillness, which both they and the spirits need. You would benefit by going to your *cave* more often.

Guard your gateways well, and be aware of the distractions too. Distractions have many faces. A distraction is so clever that it will never present itself to you with the same face twice.

The Challenges of the Mind

The mind can be a friend, but when it comes to spiritual work, it can be one's worst enemy.

It will create all kinds of stories and will tell you the most strange and bizarre things to try to sway you away from the spiritual path. But why is that? Why is the mind not in alignment with the spiritual self?

Why is it afraid, and why does it create stories that cause one to fear? Surely shouldn't one's mind be very happy to know that one has finally found one's spiritual self, that one has finally connected to one's heart and everything all around?

You see, the mind is very much connected to what the eyes can see. It only understands and accepts what can be seen with the physical eyes. If you think about it, you see that it is already a massive work for the mind to categorise, label, name, rename, and learn how things work, never mind having to remember things, people's names, people's faces, and the names of things that it learns on a daily basis. So the mind is already very busy with work and tasks. It also has to work with the body, using the neurological pathways to transmit signals from the brain to the body and from the body to the brain.

There is the right side of the brain and the left side of the brain. However, what happens to spiritual things, which are neither logical nor creative? Who works with those, the right or the left? Spiritual things are difficult for the mind because the mind is already overloaded and very busy with this and that, so the things that are not creative or logical in reality need to be worked out by the two sides of the brain working together and in harmony.

If you think of the left side of the brain and right side of the brain as muscles, you can see that they are developed according to how much one uses them, right? So what happens when one doesn't exercise these two parts of the brain to work together? One side becomes atrophied; that door is closed. To access the "spiritual brain", one needs to go through the doorway that opens when left and right are working together. Together they form a key to open another kind of brain.

It is a bit like taking a lift and going up. On the first floor we pass the logical mind; on the second floor we pass the creative mind; and to reach to the third floor, the spiritual mind, we need to pass the first and the second floors.

We need to accept the limitations of our minds on the first floor. From the first floor, it is impossible to have a full view such as that which we can have on the third floor.

The third floor, the spiritual self or spiritual mind, is able to resolve things for the first floor. It is also able to do logical things and give answers that help to satisfy the logical mind in the second floor. Equally, the spiritual mind is able to give answers and help the creative mind.

Amazing pieces are created on the second floor with inspiration coming from the third floor, the spiritual mind.

Great inventions are created on the first floor, the logical mind, with inspiration and information coming from above.

However, it is not so easy for the lower mind (first floor) to go up to the higher mind (third floor), because the lower mind is busy enough with what is going on down on the first floor. It does not quite understand that if it moves one or two levels up, it will find more resources there to be used.

Because it has not been to the third floor and seen it, because it has not catalogued it yet, the lower mind refuses to leave what it is doing to explore the spiritual realm of the third floor and gain new connections and approach new horizons. Because of the way the lower mind operates on the first floor, and because it is very rigid about the way it operates, it thinks that it will have to name more things, label more things, and catalogue more things if it goes up to the third floor, and as it is, the lower mind is already busy enough. So that is why scientists, for example, are quite happy to just stay locked where they are and do what they are doing, just processing and cataloguing information.

So what happens on the second floor, the creative mind? The mind sits quite happily there too because it has access to the first floor and the second floor, which are the logical mind and the creative mind respectively. It is aware that there is a third floor, but often it is simultaneously not quite willing to go up to explore and access the resources up there, so it waits happily for inspiration to come down from the third floor.

The human mind is by nature very lazy. To think that we only use a very small percentage of our minds is a very interesting thing.

Some scientists can have a spiritual life too, but this is definitely not the case for some. Some artists also have a spiritual life, but again such is not the case for the majority.

The problem is that we are often afraid of the forces of nature because nature is unpredictable.

The logical mind and the creative mind know that once the spiritual mind is activated, we will become one with all around us, becoming one with people, nature, and all things. When we are one with people, nature, and all things, our lives can become unpredictable too.

The farther up we go, the greater the view, and the deeper the understanding we have, the more wisdom we have too. However, the farther up we go, the more we may encounter unpredictable things in our lives.

First, we begin to lose attachment to things and people in the physical world. Second, we have to surrender control. Once our spiritual mind is activated, we begin to operate from a higher place, operating with our intuition and using a lot of other faculties and senses that we never used before, such as telepathic communication, remote viewing, and moving and changing energies at will. We have so many other faculties and senses that are yet to be discovered. Those senses can only be experienced and developed if we are willing to go up farther than the first and second floors. And who knows what we will discover if we move even farther than the third floor! Can you possibly imagine?

CHAPTER 6

Talking to Spirits—My Personal Quest to Learn about Healing

At first I felt that I had a calling to go into the forest. I got myself changed into warm clothes. It was very cold out there. When I was about to take the right turn to the forest, I heard a voice saying, "Keep walking forward."

What a beautiful place, I thought. *I am truly blessed to live here amidst all this nature and beauty that is everywhere and in everything.* Then I realised that it had been exactly one year since I had walked in this very place. I did not know where I was going. All I could hear was "Keep walking," so that is what I did.

I then decided to look for the little house that had been coming into my visions for the past year. The only thing I knew was that it was a tiny house hundreds of years old and that it was beside a river. So I decided to follow the river. The water was high and the current strong because of the snow that had been melting from the mountaintops for two days.

I came to a point where there was no other choice but to jump across the river or go back. My legs are short, so I had to look for the narrowest place to cross. My mind kept saying, *There is no way you can jump this river. Are you out of your mind?* Well, I had been trying to quieten my mind for quite a few years at that point, so I just threw my drum to the other side of the river to see what would happen. *Oh my God! Now you have to jump! You cannot leave your drum there!*

Well, that was quite easy—a good way to trick the mind, I thought.

So off I went. I flew across the river before my mind had time to say no. My skirt got wet. "Not too bad," I said, giggling. Then I had to grab the muddy bank of the river to pull myself up from the edge of the river. I picked up my drum and set off.

I was hungry, and the wind was very cold. Immediately, Mother Nature offered me something to eat. Right in front of me, there was a field of winter greens. Delicious!

My scarf became a hat, so my ears were warm now—and there I was in the middle of nowhere. I had absolutely no idea of my whereabouts.

I walked for quite some time looking for the little house which had been coming into my visions. Suddenly there it was, a tall hollow tree with a big opening in the trunk. Inside, if I stood up, there was room for my whole body. *A perfect little house,* I thought, *just like in my visions.* It was dusk; I felt the veil of darkness silently descending. In a few minutes, it would be really, really dark.

I could smell fear creeping around, trying to find its way in. *I have to be quick this time,* I thought. So I shifted and asked permission to enter the spirit world, which I did, safe and sound. I sheltered myself inside the tree; I wanted to be invisible in case fear was still creeping around. How comfortable and welcoming it was! I felt supported, deeply happy, and warm. There I stood, observing the physical world from a far place.

My quest began. A deep voice of wisdom started to speak. At first it felt like the wisdom of the tree, but then I realised it had come from beyond the familiar wisdom of my friends. I asked about something that had happened to me the day before, and I heard this in reply: "Sometimes our physical world, the world of our illusions, will collapse. Sometimes our illusions will not collapse at all, yet they will be taken away from us. This is natural, and it is a necessary thing so that one can access the world beyond the physical: the world of spirit. It is difficult to access the spiritual world if one is always grasping and grabbing at the illusions of the physical world. The world itself makes it clear that the world of spirit is not about matter or grievances. So all that is not spirit has to be left behind.

"Everyone can commune with spirits if they choose to do so," I heard. I then focused on my quest, as I was there to learn about healing. "Intent," I was told, "holds the key to your quest to learn about healing. And the importance of intent should not be taken lightly. It is very important to have a clear intent in your heart."

I walked through the forest and sat at my chosen place, looking down the river. The current was extremely strong, I felt uneasy. A part of me was afraid of the power of that flow. I thought of the flow of the universe and the many times in my life when I had fought against the flow. This made me feel uneasy too. I stood there for quite some time, very quiet and still, waiting for something but not quite sure what. I could feel my guides behind me; they were also very quiet and still.

Suddenly, from the darkness between the trees, I felt something jump from my left to my right. It was very big and black, like a really big bear. I didn't feel threatened or in danger, but I could feel the power and authority of whatever it was. It wasn't there to play or have fun; it had come to challenge me. I stood still; it did not feel appropriate to move. I kept holding to my intention to learn about healing.

The bear said, "So, you are here to learn about healing? And what makes you think we would teach you? You are weak, you have no clear intent, and you have a big ego." His words felt like a sharp knife cutting me in two. Tears poured down my face. He was right: I was weak. I didn't even know why I wanted to learn about healing. My intent was not clear, and amidst everything else, there was my ego.

I felt crushed and inadequate. I was ready to give up and go back home, when I sensed someone else watching me from about two metres away. Still crying and looking down the river, I heard the gentle and kind voice in my ears. "Why don't you go and talk to the tree you have healed? Maybe it will give you some insight into what to do."

I was tired, I couldn't see the point of going there, and to top it off, it felt like a long way to go. Just then, I heard the bear spirit again: "You see how weak you are? Do you think that knowledge will be given to you without your making any effort? If you want something, you have to act upon it. First, you have to shift from where you are, a place of weakness and victimhood."

It was really hard; my body just wanted to stay there, completely defeated. It took all my energy and willpower to stand up and walk down the little hill in the direction of the tree. My body felt ill, heavy, and in pain. I used my walking stick to help myself down. I was feeling really sorry for myself and was hoping for sympathy from my old friend the tree.

The victim within me was now so strong and heavy that the next moment my walking stick broke in two! I was shocked. The spirits of my ancestors had given me that walking stick the day before, and I had grown very fond of it. I was even a bit attached to it. I felt as if my crutch had been suddenly wrenched away from me and I had no other option but to straighten myself up and walk properly. In astonishment, I picked one half of the stick off the ground and asked Spirit, "Why? Why?"

Then I remembered the cracking noise when the stick broke and realised it had been a wake-up call for me. Suddenly, all became very clear: I had the choice to walk in beauty and power, but instead, there I was, crippled and weak. That was not good. I got myself to the tree, but there was no sympathy there to be found, not one bit. I wondered why my friend the tree, who had always been pleased to see me the many times I had come to give her a healing, was now standing there as if she didn't know me at all. I felt desolated. I curled up beneath her with tears pouring down my face. My ego could not take it any more. "What have I done wrong?" I asked.

Just then I heard the voice of the tree: "You think you are weak, and you think your ego and weakness are part of you. They are not. They are not who you are. Now get up and get yourself into that river and ask the water spirit to wash away your ego and your weakness. Offer your ego and your weakness to the water spirit."

I looked at the river. Surely the current was too powerful? It felt as if too much was being asked of me, but at the same time, I knew what I had to do. I had come many times to that same river and had asked it to remove dead, lethargic, diseased energies from my body. So many times had I gone there, removed my socks, and immersed my feet in the river. The water spirit would always happily cleanse my body and energy system, leaving me vibrant and strong once again.

I stood up. I still had the two pieces of crutch in my hands, so I used them to help myself down from the bank into the river, where I tested the depth of the water. It was very cold. I felt the urge to move right into the current and let its power do the cleansing. Suddenly I could feel the strength of the water pushing at me. I had to stand firmly on my feet so as not to succumb to its power. I saw my weaknesses being washed away, together with the two pieces of crutch. I asked Spirit to wash away my ego too. My wellington boots were filled with water—the water of Spirit! I started to laugh and laugh, feeling much lighter and content.

I climbed out of the river, removed my wellington boots, emptied out the water, and felt really strong and empowered. As I walked up the little hill, I felt a great happiness come over me. As I passed by the place where I had encountered the bear spirit, I felt very proud of myself and thought, *Well, I am strong now, very strong!*

At once I heard, "Come back tomorrow then, to get rid of your self-importance."

Dona Mercedes, My First Teacher at Age Thirteen

I look down upon my body to observe a Brazilian woman fully dressed in white. My skirt is not fashionable; it is simple, plain white, ankle length—ceremonial style. My top is perhaps a little more fashionable.

I chose it myself, a netted top with little white daisies. Daisies are my preferred flower. Around my head, I am wearing a bandanna made of colourful tiny feathers held in a circle by bamboo. I like it. The colour is bright. Not only is it practical in that it keeps my hair away from my eyes, but also it takes me back to my South American roots. I feel much more connected to my roots, to whom I truly am. The bandanna gathers my thoughts and energy inside.

As my spirit gazes upon her body, from above I see this woman who is a stranger to me yet is very familiar. It is as if I have gone back to the time of no time. I actually need some real time to adjust to what I see. Have I truly become a *curandera*, a healer, a shaman-healer? The way I look, the way I walk, the way I pray, the way I live my life, living far away up in the mountains, far from people, is either a sign that I have gone totally mad, as I so feared before, or a confirmation that I have truly become a healer.

My heart pounds with joy. Secretly I laugh. I have worked very hard to move to another country and learn another language. I have worked relentlessly to eradicate poverty from my life and from the lives of others. I have left behind family and dear friends. I have changed my life completely. Twenty-six years have passed. And there I am, back to my own roots again, this time with even greater strength. One can run away from family, other people, and places, but one can never run away from the self, the real self. I laugh within.

I am proud of who I am. I am proud to be reconnected to my indigenous roots and able to help so many people who come to my door where I am, hidden away up in the mountains. People come because they suffer from spiritual, emotional, mental and sometimes physical diseases too.

My hands began to work. They moved up and down and all around the aura of this six-foot-tall man, just like Dona Mercedes my teacher used to do. I then had the thought that perhaps I had become just like Dona Mercedes herself. Was it my hands doing the work or was it hers?

When I was nine years old, my parents moved to the suburbs of São Paulo. This involved a move from the centre of one of the biggest cities in the world to a small town three hours away. Dona Mercedes was a wise woman in her seventies; she was a neighbour and like a grandmother to me. She lived with her husband, with their daughter-in-law and two young granddaughters next door. Her son, who was very young, had died from cancer six months before we moved next door to her. The family were still grieving when this little girl with long black hair and so much sadness in her eyes moved next to them. The sadness was so deep that it was not possible for it to have come from only this life. It must have come from many lives before. So Dona Mercedes, still grieving for her son, adopted this little girl as if one of her own granddaughters; she became my first teacher.

It took a few years for the bond to grow. My mother was bipolar and mentally ill every two years, and spiritual help was always considered as an option when mother was suffering. Dona Mercedes was always called in to remove the spirits that would always attach themselves to my mother. She would remove the feelings of despair and hopelessness that always accompanied my mother's crises, like a shadow descending over the family.

Dona Mercedes was kind. She had a fragile body, but her spirit was like a powerful rock. When she died twenty years later, her spirit flew as birds do and she glided quietly away to the spirit world. No fuss, no noise, no crisis. That is how medicine people go, how they leave the physical world. They are like birds, leaving no trace behind, but if you are paying attention, you can feel their spirits around you. They come at moments of crisis; they come to comfort the sick and the ill. That is who they are, and that is why they are called medicine people.

Soul Retrieval for the Self

For me to be able to work with others, I need to continuously work on myself. So I search for the lost parts of my soul—a forever spiritual journey of healing.

I ask Spirit what soul parts I need back right now. The answer comes loud and clear: mental health and the child. Mental illness used to run in my family, generation after generation, until now. Mother, Grandmother, and Great-Grandmother have all suffered and inflicted suffering onto others. The child part of my soul had fled as far away as she could go. Now it was time to bring her back home, home to the safety and sanctity of the body, mind, and spirit.

The spirit of the hummingbird came to help. The hummingbird knows of unconditional love and knows what medicine the child needs. So the journey began, the journey to encounter the soul parts that I needed back right now.

The three of us children were going up the steps to a long narrow garden entrance. We were greeted by a kind woman, her eyes showing mercy and kindness. Her husband was also kind and gentle. They could not have children themselves. So when they heard of the three of us, aged six, five, and four, without a mother, they were quickly ready to give all they had: a clean bed, food on time to cease the hunger, clean clothes, and most importantly love.

Being only six, I could not quite understand why Mother had left. Did she no longer love us? Why did she have to go? Nobody explained what happened. All I knew was that Mother was gone again. So on that night, I sat and cried. I cried very hard and sobbed. Inside I felt empty and sad. Would Mother ever return? A day was too long. A week was unbearable. A month, two months, three months, sometimes six months would pass and I would still not know what had happened to my mother. Who had taken Mother away?

What about my brother and my sister? They also felt the same pain, the same anguish. Deep inside, what connected and still connects the three of us is the terrible pain of loss we shared. What I did not know was that the pain I still feel deep inside myself to this day is the pain of mourning. I am mourning the loss of my mother, the hummingbird explained.

Now I could understand why I never felt happy. Life is so beautiful and life is complete, yet life is not joyful. Hummingbird explained that every two years when my mother went to the hospital, my child self suffered the same loss that a child suffers when a mother dies. So I pick up the sobbing child from the bed and hold her in my arms with great tenderness, embracing her with a love beyond existence.

Can I protect this child from the harshness of life? Can I protect this child from the cruelty of life? Can I change what has gone before? I need to bring the child from the dimension of suffering and trauma back to the here and now, back to safety. But the child, who has always been conscious of the suffering of others, will not leave without her brother and sister. Brother, who has suffered immensely in childhood, often drinks himself to sleep, to forget. Sister, who has cried and cried inconsolably, works herself to death so she can forget. Not forgive, but forget. I am sad. I cannot leave my brother and sister's soul parts there in that bed, even though the woman is lovely, the man is kind, and they have no children of their own. So without a second thought, I grab my sister by the hand, I grab my brother by the hand, and like a swirl we fly out the door, leaving behind the pain that united the three of us in sadness. I blow their soul parts back into their bodies and then blow my own soul part back into my own heart.

The childlike heart has returned home. What I did not know was that for two days I would be totally wiped out without energy or enthusiasm, just a sleepy soul tired of sobbing and tired of mourning. I was not prepared to see how weak my energy body was: for two days I was constantly falling asleep, barely able to hold myself up. And that is a true story.

Rites of Passage for Women

I arrived at twelve noon, never having managed to arrive early for anything. I have pondered about this many times. Medicine people are never on time. That is because we are not bound by time: time is bound by us. There was no time to think about it now; I had to open the Planetary Healing Centre, carry all my stuff in, and set the table for lunch, because after all food is really important. I laughed.

The women gathered in the sacred circle. They had arrived one by one, carrying their flowers. I noticed one wise woman sitting in the circle. She was the oldest one. Wise women are always quiet. They speak only when it is necessary, and they are always ready to help others. They have moved beyond the self, and on their horizon, others are much more important.

We opened the sacred circle and called the ancestral women to witness the death of their daughters and their granddaughters, for they were there to die. They were there to let go of their old selves. They were there because they had had enough. They were there to cross the threshold to enter the way beyond this way. I was their guide who would take them across the threshold. I had been called to be their death celebrant, to give them their last rites, for they were ready to be born again. But for one to be born again, one must first die. Seven women entered the circle of power, eight if we're counting me. There was silence first, then there were tears, then there was laughter, and then there was silence again.

Life always brings to us all the initiations we need, but sometimes it is better to be one step ahead of life and create conscious initiations ourselves. It is always better to create the life we want than to just let life happen to us. I thought that and spoke it out loud. I am less and less afraid to speak these days because I only speak the truth. The deeper I go into the truth, the easier it is to do my work.

I took a deep breath, amongst the tears, and also felt excitement. This is always the way with death: beyond death, there is always excitement.

And so the sacred rites began. One by one the women spoke of the lives, the families, and the relations they were leaving behind. Great sadness entered the room.

I had known that the work was not going to be easy. I had to be strong myself to hold such a space. On the agenda was a sacred rites ceremony, a ceremony of unravelling the self, a sound journey, a death ceremony, the rebirth, and then the celebration.

When the women emerged from their deaths, having left all that no longer served them behind, they cried, and their tears were truthful. I knew they were ready to begin to live again, this time conscious, this time stronger.

They were like Amazon warrior women: for one to be ready to fully live, one must be ready to die.

Past Life and Beyond

I held his lifeless body in my arms. His spirit had fled; the pain in his physical body was no more. The anger and sadness were no more. The illusion that he no longer had to feel his heart was strong. He would never again need to look into the eyes of his beloved and feel the pain of betrayal. Leaving this world was easy; taking his own life was easy. Blood was pouring down into the earth, the earth that would now take his body while his spirit was free.

Now he was free, but free from what? Free from his own heart? from himself? from the turmoil that tortured his mind? Where would his spirit go? Would his spirit remember? He did not know; he did not want to remember; he wanted to forget.

In the land of Spirit, I held him, and in my heart I felt infinite compassion. My heart was open, and I felt his pain. A whirling of deep compassion surrounded his body. It is common for me to enter ethereal realms and have spirals of colourful energy follow me. What medicine was needed to heal his soul? The wounds were deep; his spirit was gone. How could I bring back his spirit, as he no longer wanted to be?

His beloved was there too. She sat in desolation, tears pouring down her face. She felt guilty and ashamed. How could she have betrayed him that way? How could she embrace another, give her body to another, in such betrayal? Her heart was broken. Her spirit was broken. Now that he had taken his own life, she would carry within herself the mark of betrayal forever; there was no way back. There was nothing she could do to make amends. There were no more promises to be broken.

I thought deeply about what to do. This man had come to me asking to be fully in his body. Somehow he felt it was time to ask for my help, apparently because he knew I could help him. He had wandered for life after life seeking to be in his body and somehow had become overwhelmed by the feelings of anger and sadness within. He could not remember why he was so angry or why he was so sad, and he could not understand why he could not be fully in his body. He had been gifted with many abilities, including a full connection with lucid dreams, something that many people dream to have and work very hard to acquire

With a deep authority from within, I called his spirit. "It is time to stop wondering," I said. "It is time to return home, look into the eyes of your beloved, make love, and feel the pleasures of the body. Because love has fledged from your heart, anger and sadness have inundated it. But you have a choice as we all have a choice: you can carry on suffering and in pain for life after life, or you can come home to where you belong and fill your heart with love once again. Forgive and forget."

His spirit was tired of wandering, and the anger and sadness were too much to bear. He wanted to move on and to love again. What would become of the many people he had helped in this life if he failed to return home to himself? What would become of the suffering souls coming to seek his help? If his heart is filled with anger and sadness, what did he have to offer these people? Yes, he was ready. His mind was not, but in his heart of hearts, he knew what he had to do.

As fast as lightning, I held his soul in my hands and blew it back into his heart. His beloved found her way in, as the gateway between the worlds was still open. *Can she do that? Should I allow that?* It was very fast, and the vibration of the mind cannot penetrate these worlds. In my heart, I felt the love between the two of them. How could I separate two lovers? The love of the beloved and the love of the lover are one. Their hearts are one, and their spirits are one. Love is beyond comprehension. Love is beyond life itself. We all seek in another our own divine selves.

A new memory came in. It was as if life had begun again. Like a new baby feeling its way into the body, out of the womb, this man was shivering. Ready to take the first breath of life, his spirit entered his body fully.

What changes will come? I wondered inside myself. My work was completed. It was not easy, but it was completed. His spirit had wandered for a very long time, perhaps many lives, who knows! It had once taken shelter in a white eagle. The white eagle holds many symbols, along with answers and wisdom. The spiral was revealed as one of the sacred symbols. This man's journey would continue now that he had been reconnected to his body. The eagle was his medicine, his totem animal spirit. The spiral was a repeated message about feeling his path with his feet. Being grounded and present, and holding strength, power, and wisdom in his body, was a requirement for where he is now, serving his people.

I thanked the spirits, for without them this work could not have been done. Without them, I could not have entered the spirit world and returned unharmed.

I looked towards the east and thanked the spirit of fire, as fire would melt his sadness and turn it into love. I looked into the south and thanked the spirit of water, as water would cleanse his heart and allow love to flow again. I looked into the west and thanked the spirit of earth, as the earth would compost anger into acceptance. I looked into the north and thanked the spirit of air, as air would bring new memories into his mind. I looked into the above and thanked the spirits of above for giving me the ability to look beyond the self, which is always needed to move forward in life. I looked into the below and thanked the spirits of below for the good, strong support they had given me. I felt held and loved. I looked within and thanked the spirits of within. In doing so, I found peace, clarity and harmony. I had brought harmony back to his heart and brought balance back to his life.

Then, secretly laughing, I thought, *People don't really know how they develop these diseases of the spirit.*

CHAPTER 7

Well-Being and Healing

The chemotherapy this week was not so bad; there was no nausea, or tiredness, or anything like that. She was feeling strong, which is why she was here sitting in front of me once again. Her spine was not so good though; the pain sometimes could be unbearable. The doctors had done what they could. They were surprised when the last test result showed that both tumours had shrunk.

I went closer, looked piercingly into her eyes, and asked, "Hmm, where is this coming from? Let's go back in time. Have you had any problems with your spine before? When did it start?" She jolted in disbelief and some form of excitement, as she knew we were getting to the root of the problem. She could remember the exact day and time when she was dropped and fell on her spine. Since that day, she never felt right again.

The tumours in her neck were fine; the doctors said they were shrinking. However, I wanted to look deeper. I always look deeper, never convinced that what is before me is real. My eyesight has been going for a while. The worse it gets, the more I can see in the spirit world.

I peered and peered into the spirit world. I saw the child, the desolated child, the poor child. I sensed overwhelming feelings of not being loved, of not being seen, of being isolated. So I called the child: "Come back home to yourself. Come back strong and loved. Come back to be seen.

Your strength is needed. Your love is needed. Come to stand tall. Come to stand strong. We all want to be loved; we all want to be seen; and we all yearn for a place under the sun, a place in the world." When I got the child, I blew her back into my client's spine.

Then I peered again. A gallant soldier appeared on his tall white horse. He had a sword in his hand and was wearing a red uniform. His heart was empty; he killed without thought; and his sword pierced many bodies, so many that he could not count. He was tired and weary. He no longer knew for whom he fought, why he fought, or who he was. I knew this was beyond my abilities: war, killings, swords. Grandfather was called, and when he came, he brought the song of balance, the song of harmony and remembering. "Come and sit with Grandfather," he said to the gallant soldier. "Come and listen to your heart. We must not fight for one; we must fight for all. When your sword pierces another, your sword is piercing your own self. Your sword is piercing your own soul. Let Grandfather put you together." And then he sang the song of healing, the song of balance, for what felt like an eternity. Harmony returned and peace entered the warrior's heart.

The tree was tall. The buds were beginning to come out and stretch themselves like they do in the spring. But I knew that the spirit of this disease was not like any other. I had to be strong; I had to be truthful; I had to come from my heart or this spirit would close himself to me. I knew my request was a big one. I knew that what I was about to ask was no small thing. For one to ask something of a majestic one, one needs to be majestic herself. So I kept coming from my heart. "Hello, majestic one. I hear you come from a faraway land. I hear you are tall and strong. I see your power. I see your strength. I have a request to make of you. Could you go to sleep? Could you go for a long rest? I know you want to stretch and grow. I have nothing to give you. I cannot offer you anything, but I am requesting from my heart to yours. My friend suffers when you grow. Please take your buds inside. Go deep within, rest, and sleep."

So it was that a giant was put to sleep simply by the powers of the heart and the heart alone. I then smiled. "Let it dream me and you for a while."

121

The Glow of a Pregnant Woman

Her hair was beautiful; in it were beautiful feathers. She was aglow with the glow of a pregnant woman. Women who hold life inside glow so powerfully that it is startling to others to see. Her belly was huge; she could barely stand up and walk. How intelligent life is, and how powerful women are for creating life, nourishing another being, and loving unconditionally. Her belly was round and colourful. And when she smiled, it was as if the world was blessed by her smile. Her man was there too. He sat proud and very happy beside her.

The circle was completed. All those who had touched her life in some ways were there: sisters, brothers, grandmothers, friends. In the sacred circle, a deeper bond was created by this spirit who would arrive by the next full moon. His powers could already be seen if one looked with the heart. White flowers, the symbol of purity, decorated the centre. Tobacco prayers, hundreds of them, were brought ceremonially to the centre. We all sat quietly in the circle of sisters, brothers, grandmothers, and friends.

Prayers began to emerge from each person's heart, prayers of gratitude, of health, of welcoming, of joy. The sacred peace pipe was filled with those prayers, and in the great smoke the prayers flowed to the Great Spirit. The Great Spirit would hear them, for they carried the vibration of the heart.

The soul would make a safe passage into the physical world. It would continue its journey of growth and spiritual development. It had chosen wise parents, spiritual warriors who would teach by being. And his spiritual journey would be nourished by a community that was bonded and made stronger, just by the thought of his arrival.

The Language of the Heart—a Meditation

The labyrinth of the heart can be difficult to navigate sometimes. Those who hold love and compassion in their hearts receive the map of heart wisdom. Heart wisdom is the ability to touch that which is invisible, to touch that which is powerful, and to touch that which is graceful. It lies in the heart and the heart alone.

The legacy entrusted to us humans, but one which we so often fail to recognise, is the power of the heart. Creativity comes from the heart, and healing comes from the heart. The power to create peace comes from the heart. Therefore, when the heart closes, it makes way for intolerance, anger, aggression, and war to arise.

Yoga, meditation, tai chi, magical passes, and dance are some of the many ways given to us which help to open up the heart. Though a simple yet profound way to begin is to practise this short meditation:

> Sit comfortably in a place where you will not be disturbed, with both feet resting on the floor or ground and your knees a little apart. Your spine must be upright so that all your chakras are in alignment. Either place your hands, palms up, on your lap or rest them lightly on your kneecaps.
>
> Visualise the colour of rose quartz and bring it to your heart. Resonate with that colour, experiencing your heart glowing with the warmth of the rose quartz. Now let that colour flow into your entire body. Deepen the colour with every breath. As you do so, your breathing will automatically start to slow down. The resonance and vibration of love in the heart will begin to grow and strengthen. Hold that resonance of love within the core of your being, within your heart, and in the palm of your hands, thereby making an offering.
>
> Think of those people in your life who bring challenges to you now and again. Take that rose quartz light to them,

because they need that love and healing too. Think of the ones who are more challenging than others. As you grow in your love, your rose quartz light will expand within you, touching even those who present you with your greatest challenge.

Be aware of the light moving up to your head, where it has the power to dissolve the mental barriers between you and the one with whom you are in conflict.

Do not be afraid to love! If you are finding it difficult to release the blockages within your heart, just repeat this meditation each day until you succeed.

When the heart has found release, you will be ready to move to the next stage. Now attune your consciousness to an elevated level by visualising Goddess consciousness or Christ, Buddha, Kwan-Yin, Virgin Mary, Krishna, Allah, or any other High Consciousness that resonates with you—a consciousness that can hold the eternal flame of unconditional love and compassion.

In shamanism, we say that the way to change the world out there is to change the world within, sending healing, bringing our own vibration to its highest level, and resonating with peace, purity, and compassion.

The word we must treasure is *compassion*. I invite you to put that word into action today.

The Home of the Self

The home of the self, the divine wisdom inspired from above, comes to you through your vocal cords, through your hands, and through your heart and soul, to alleviate suffering everywhere, to untangle what has been tangled, and to bring hope for the future. This divine wisdom from above is invoked in the service of love.

To open the connection between humankind and God, open your heart and body, open your mind and thoughts, and let the divine message pour through you.

Welcome from the realm of spirit. You are in the process of discovering the magnitude of the self, your true self. The magnitude of the true self of all humanity is likewise in the process of discovery. The light has come. The wisdom has come for those who have been seeking. It has come from above as it has come from below. The place of wisdom is the place of the heart.

Welcome from the realm of the heart. To touch without heart and to reach without wisdom is not to touch and not to reach at all. Trust yourself, for it is through this trust that wisdom will come. You must first become strong. You must also gather patience, because patience is power. Those who reside in the realms of the divine are happy to talk to you and happy to talk through you. Open to more light, as more light is needed. Invoke more power, for more power is needed. Others will arrive in due course, when the time is right. You must decide what your subject is and develop your focus, because a great deal of focus is also needed. Be aware that Spirit is working right now within you, opening the channel.

Divine Mother, Divine Wisdom, the Light of all Times, is within us. She has never left. There is the time of the Warrior, of male energy, and there is the time of the Divine Mother, the healer. What we are seeing now is the return of the Divine Mother; the wisdom coming through is the wisdom of the Divine Mother. However, the Warrior needs to be there too, to protect her and to open the path for her to walk in beauty. This is a divine law; it is the way it is and the way it has always been. The balance of the male and female energies within has not come about by chance, as there is divine law behind everything.

An epoch of great wisdom is approaching. We have passed the age of industrialisation, are completing the age of information, and are now approaching the age of wisdom. With the age of wisdom will come the age of manifestation. Because, as has been the case with every great age that has gone before, the soul yearns to manifest. The time will come when miracles will be commonplace. With the manifestation of clarity, the manifestation of wisdom, and the manifestation of love, all will be possible. However, before that can happen, there is work to be done.

A Personal Prayer for My Funeral: Gratitude to Our Earth Mother

To our blessed Mother Earth, I know you can hear me. I know you can hear what is in my heart, spirit, and soul.

Deep gratitude, Mother. Deep gratitude for the rivers you give us unpolluted and that in my ignorance I polluted.

Deep gratitude for the air that fills up my lungs, the air that only you can provide, that only you can generate with such precision and care. Again, in my ignorance, I polluted it.

A prayer of gratitude for the trees, the bushes, the little greens, the grass, the flowers, the bees. In my ignorance, I killed them.

A prayer of gratitude for the children who play and laugh, and for our elders who grow wise and slow. A prayer of gratitude for the animals who walked beside me on this earth.

Mother, for me to get to this place of gratitude, I had to find love in my heart. I had to cross the oceans to see your beauty and learn to admire you.

Mother, my walking feet rest now. They have blessed me, taking me to many places of unbelievable beauty and peace.

Mother, touch my spirit even deeper. Take me closer to you. Next life, teach me how not to pollute, how not to be greedy. Show me, Mother, that I am safe, that you take care of me, that you always provide for me and will always do so. All I need to do is to rest in your arms and receive from your gentle heart.

When I take my last breath, Mother, may it be a peaceful breath. May it be a breath filled with love, your love, Mother. When finally my body lies down into your being to rest, may my rest be a peaceful rest filled with your love, Mother, held by you to the end.

Mother, forgive me for the times I did not pick up enough rubbish from you. Forgive me for the times I did not respect you enough. Mother, forgive me for the times I was greedy, for I was a little child, small, afraid, and lost.

Mother, I have grown to know you, I have come closer to you, I have rested many times in peace with you. To the end, Mother, I will always be close to you.

May all the children I have played with on this earth also come close to you, Mother, and feel what I felt with you: safe, loved, cared for, provided for.

In love and deep gratitude,
Cláudia Gonçalves

CHAPTER 8

My Experience of the Vision Quest

The vision quest marks an ending and brings new beginnings. That is what justifies it as a rite of passage, a moving on from one thing to another.

The vision quest is as old as humankind. The very act of going away to sit in silence and contemplation has been part of every culture and civilisation that has gone before and will be part of every culture and civilisation that springs up on earth after we are gone. We go to nature to receive insights into something. Often the insights are about our lives and our purpose for being here. We go away from the hustle and bustle of our lives to receive guidance, understanding, and wisdom. No people, food, or comfort will distract us during the four days and four nights of the vision quest.

A vision quest is not to be taken lightly; it is not another tick in a box to say, "I have done it!" No. A vision quest is an old tradition that deserves deep respect. When we approach it with respect, the spirit of vision quest will help us in infinite ways with answers.

Spirits are our guides in the spirit world. The vision quest guide is our guide in the physical world. Nature is our guide and is the bridge between the two worlds. If we find things are difficult for us to face on our own, we can return and receive counsel in the physical world from our vision quest guide. Sometimes we just need someone to listen to us in order for healing to take place; we talk about what troubles us and then return to our vision quest. Seeking help to deal with things is part of taking responsibility and empowering ourselves.

Mainly for safety reasons, it is not advisable to do a vision quest by venturing on one's own deep into the wilderness. Also, as part of our healing, it is important to have a community who greet us on our return, a community of people who witness what we go through and who welcome us back into this life as we're returning from the spirit world as a new, stronger person. Even if that community is just our vision quest guide, it is important for us to be witnessed and held when we return from the spirit world.

I would like to share with you a little bit of my experience with the vision quest. What I share here is a glimpse of my understanding of performing and being held in this sacred ceremony. I also recommend *The Book of the Vision Quest: Personal Transformation in the Wilderness* and *The Roaring of the Sacred River: The Wilderness Quest for Vision and Self-Healing*, both of which are written by Steven Foster and Meredith Little from the School of Lost Borders.

A vision quest requires us to be in nature for four days and nights, spent fasting and communing with the spirits, who provide direction and point the way towards some deep and profound changes in our lives.

I live my spiritual life in trust because I know that Spirit has plans. And because I am a little mouse, I can only see a glimpse of Spirit's plans. Therefore, I have learnt to live my life in complete trust on this path.

Living in trust is not an easy thing. The south of our personal wheel of life teaches us that living in the trust is necessary for walking a spiritual path. As for me, things will usually unfold when I allow them to, before my very own eyes—without controlling it.

When we are in nature for the four days and four nights, the weather can be a mirror of how we are feeling within. Our relationship with the weather during the vision quest can tell us a lot about what is going on inside ourselves.

Four days and four nights of fasting in the wilderness is necessary for us to cover four aspects of ourselves: south (our emotions), west (our body), north (our mind), and east (our spirit). These directions are called the *four shields* or *medicine shields*.

Sometimes the vision quester needs to adapt to practical things, depending on the country where he or she is doing the vision quest. For example, only two months offer a window for a vision quest in Scotland, where the weather can be harsh. Naturally, the vision quester needs to prepare for cold conditions, even during summer. Once, one of those life-saving bags insulated with aluminium came to my rescue during a vision quest. I am eternally grateful for it as it was a very cold night in Scotland, despite the fact that it was summertime.

The rest of the year in Scotland would present the vision quester with a fight for survival. And if one is fighting to survive, one will find it very hard to go deep into the spiritual work.

Depending on where you are on the globe, you will need different things. It is good to be prepared. The worst thing is to be cold during the night as the vision quester is not to leave his or her place. Being too cold can be reason enough for giving up. Therefore, go well prepared for survival. Most people fear hunger, but usually the vision quester is a little hungry on the first day only. As one enters the second day of fasting, the body no longer feels hungry and food is the last thing one thinks of. It is important that the vision quester be responsible for himself or herself, knowing his or her limitations and taking care of his or her safety at all times.

If rain is expected, put up a tarpaulin to keep dry. It's important to keep your clothes and sleeping bags dry because things can become hard if you are wet and cold. If, like me, you have low blood sugar, then taking a little honey might be a good idea to keep the hummingbird inside alive.

You also need to make sure you are not doing your quest in areas where protected animals live, so you do not disturb them.

Only drink water from local streams if you know it is safe to do so or if you are experienced and know how to purify water.

130

You must have a "container"—someone to hold you energetically while you quest. A trained vision quest guide would be ideal. If you cannot find one, then you can invite a friend you trust to be your "container" and hold space for you in the physical world. An elder would be ideal, as elders hold wisdom in them. Through their life experiences, they have gained that wisdom.

As one enters the vision quest, one dedicates the first day to the south shield, the child within, the place of emotion, the place of love, healing, and trust. One dedicates the second day to the west shield, the teenager within, the place related to the body, the place of introspection and strength. One dedicates the third day to the north shield, the adult within, the place of the mind, the place of wisdom and clarity. One dedicates the last day to the east shield, the spirit within, the place of transformation and illumination of the spiritual self.

At the end of the vision quest, one finishes in the east, as it also represents new beginnings and shows that the circle of one's human life is completed. In the circle of life, there is no beginning and no end. Where something ends, something else begins. We honour that in everything, including in death. Death is not our end; the death of the body is the beginning of something new for the spirit.

It is important to begin your quest with intent. As the quest unfolds, so too does one's intent, which undergoes a deepening. As your consciousness expands during the four days, you then begin to see the true reason why you needed and wanted to participate in a vision quest ceremony in the first place. Things start to become clear. By the end of the quest, you will be able to see the bigger picture.

When you are doing a vision quest, it is important to have someone, for example a buddy, holding space for you. That means having someone there to make sure you are safe on all levels: spiritual, physical, mental, and energetic. It is important this person knows where you are in case he or she needs to reach you or, equally, if you need to reach them, for example if an emergency arises from your side. You can achieve this without interfering with your sacred space or your silence during the deep work you do during the four days.

You can create a system where at some point your buddy will come to check on you.

To create a simple safety system, collect about three stones and pile them up. Go to the pile in the morning as a sign that all is OK with you. Your buddy will go there and take the stones down as a sign that the message has been received that you are safe and well, that you are OK. This system also works if you or your buddy needs to leave a message.

Four days of fasting can make a person very weak, unable to walk fast or for long distances. Therefore, having someone who knows where you are is really important. It is a good idea to also choose a place that is not too far and that you are able to reach help if needed.

The way one relates to nature is really important. Asking permission to enter nature is paramount. The spot one chooses is home to other creatures. One does not just arrive and enter someone's home without announcing. Creatures live there. It is also important that one enter the vision quest space quietly, with deep respect and reverence. Nature reciprocates to us when we enter with respect and reverence, and this reciprocation is a sign that we are learning to live in harmony with all things and creatures. Silence and quietness belong to nature, so one enters that silence and quietness within oneself too. One goes to nature to heal oneself, commune with her, and bring peace back to one's heart and life. Sitting in nature and being in nature is a healthy way of being. Purpose and ceremony brings another spiritual level into our lives. The vision quest is a healing ceremony.

While we are there in our natural spot, we observe all the dramas that we usually create in our lives and in our minds, and we take time to heal those dramas. The vision quest is an opportunity to notice them and make a conscious decision to no longer have drama around us or within us.

The vision quest is also an opportunity for us to look into our lives and take stock, coming to realise what is working and what is not. We heal what needs healing and make a conscious commitment to ourselves, the world around us, and future generations. While we are there, we have an opportunity to stop the world for a moment or two, reevaluate our lives, and deepen our spiritual connection.

It is humankind's birthright to go to nature, to sit, to come closer to the Mother, to listen, and to heal. It should not be a difficult experience, and there should be no hardship attached to it. For those are dramas we carry, we go to the Mother to release them and heal ourselves within. The experience should be a beautiful experience indeed, a rewarding experience for us and everyone around us. Our vision quest should enrich our lives and the lives of others around us. For this is how nature works, by healing her children and letting them feel less separated. By being close to nature and entering the realm of spirit, we heal ourselves. We become more joyful, more loving, and more compassionate human beings. We must always remember to look at the sunrise and the sunset and feel that we are loved.

Before one goes on a vision quest, one will benefit from learning how to make a small fire in nature while causing her no harm. Fire has accompanied humankind from the beginning of time. It gives us all we need, including warmth and a way to cook our food, and it teaches us about respect. Grandfather Fire is a great teacher to have with us while we are in nature.

Your fire needs to be a very small fire. It is a symbolic fire that should not burn all the time on the quest. There are many reasons for this: safety first, and you do not want the smoke to startle people who will come to your sacred space to help put a fire out! You want to be undisturbed for those four days and four nights.

At the end of your quest, put the stones you used for your little fire back where they came from and thank them. Upon leaving your natural spot, determine to leave your space as you found it, as that is a sign of respect for nature.

A little fire is a spirit helper in one's quest. It helps one to deal with Mr Boredom when he comes to pay a visit. It also keeps the inner child happy when one is working with south medicine. A little fire can also be a great focal point for meditation and contemplation in the north. If it is not possible to make a little fire for whatever reason, one can light a small candle; the fire spirit can come through the candle to help the vision quester in the same way.

During a vision quest, the quester will drink lots of water, five to ten litres, if not more. Some traditions do not allow for drinking water during a vision quest, so it will depend on your teacher. Jesus stayed in the desert for forty days and forty nights on his vision quest, and I have friends who have done forty days and forty nights without food or water. That is extreme, but it shows it is possible. A vision quest is not about testing oneself to the extremes; it is about sitting in quietness, in nature, and listening to the spirit of all things to find answers and direction.

In your spot in nature, you can find the true meaning of your life and perhaps begin to remember the reason why you came to this earth at this time. In nature, you have the opportunity to put right what is wrong, to bring balance and sanity once more into your life. In doing this, you find direction and purpose.

We were born with the instinct to survive in nature, and when we quest for four days and four nights, we are going back to our primitive selves and our earliest memories, the memory of being at peace—no matter where we are, no matter what is going on in our lives. The vision quest puts us in touch with our pure and truthful essence: the essence of a human being.

Sometimes we create a kind of vision quest in our lives subconsciously. We create diseases that make us stop the world for a while. Everything has to be on hold while we lie in bed or in a hospital somewhere reevaluating our lives. It is a natural cycle of human life to reach beginnings and endings. Perhaps if we would bring ourselves to sit silently on the earth, consciously evaluating our lives, from time to time, we would save ourselves a great deal of trouble and grievances.

There is no right or wrong; life just is as it is. However, it surely goes without saying that we would benefit from tapping into ancient ways to bring more balance and harmony into our lives today.

We are plagued with diseases because we have become disconnected from the earth. We no longer plant our own food, and those who are not vegetarian no longer hunt their own meat. We live a very boring life of going to the supermarket to get our food off the shelves, and we find ourselves depressed and unhappy. Our modern way of life does not give us a sparkle in our hearts or the smile and feelings that come from being connected and truly belonging. However, we can still recreate some old ways to rebalance the self and fill our lives with a sense of purpose and accomplishment again. A vision quest helps us to do just that when we enter into it with the right intention.

The world is filled with ancient knowledge for us to tap into. It is my belief that all ancient knowledge belongs to all the people of the earth. Tapping into ancient knowledge and remembering it is all that is required for us to live a life that is in alignment with the highest and that respects our Earth Mother.

What the Great Spirit has left on the earth is for humankind to share. As human beings, we need to resolve our differences by healing the separation in ourselves. The thought that each of us was born of one particular race or culture makes us separated. There is only one race, and that is humanity. By not claiming anything, we find that we do not have to explain anything.

Day 1: The South

The first day of the quest, look into the south of our circle of human life. Physically sitting and looking to the south allows you to fully focus on that direction and not be distracted. If you do not have a compass, you can position yourself by orienting with the sun. Knowing that the sun rises in the east and sets in the west helps you define where the south and the north is.

With the south in your consciousness, everything that will unfold on that day will relate to the south of your personal circle of life.

The element of the south is water, representing the emotions. South is the place of the child within, and as such, it is also the place of love, healing, and trust. Our emotions are like water; sometimes they flow, and sometimes they gets stuck or stale. The child within feels everything; it has no reason, only feelings.

You could begin by checking within to see how your inner child is feeling. Do you feel happy within, or do you feel sad? Tapping into the energy of the south requires you to be in touch with your emotions and feelings to identify how you relate to others emotionally. Do you relate to others from a wounded place? from a place of lack? from a place of mistrust? If so, your south shield needs work.

Sitting in a vision quest while looking into the south and feeling the emotions, allowing them to come, is a powerful way to heal the inner child within you.

Enjoying life and enjoying your work is a sign that the south of your medicine shield is healthy. Trusting and taking it easy is also a good healthy sign.

By consciously dedicating the first day of one's quest to the south, everything that happens on that day becomes an opportunity for healing.

To bring balance to yourself, you need to check if your south shield needs balance. Take time to laugh and have fun in your day-to-day work; take time for contemplation and self-healing in your day-to-day life.

The south is in opposition to the north. That means the north, one's adult self, can have a great influence on one's emotions because the north is directly related to the emotions. With well-balanced shields, one has the ability to gradually heal the wounds, gently and consciously, of one's childhood. Every time the adult self takes time to rest, relax, and play, it is healing and nurturing to the child within.

Inspiration, joy, and a sense of fulfilment come from the south to the adult self. Without a fulfilled inner child, an adult cannot have a fulfilled life. For it is the child in us who governs our emotions—and the feeling of fulfilment is an emotion.

For one to sit in a vision quest, look into the south, and heal one's childhood wounds, one needs to trust and be open. One must trust that one is being guided by Spirit. Trust in the Spirit's gentle blessing from the south with the knowledge that this blessing can then be shared with others for their healing.

Through the axis of south and north within you, it is possible to find that trust. Through trust, the adult self will share knowledge and will connect with feelings, which in turn become healing for others. Without our emotions, we are like zombies. Without emotions we are like the walking dead.

The child within shares and gives. For one's adult self to be a giver, the child within needs to be happy. It is through happiness that one gives to others. However, the child is only happy to give if he or she feels abundance. Abundant thoughts of love create love; abundant thoughts of material things create material things. We need to align ourselves with thoughts of abundance.

The child in the south is the one able to manifest. For us to be able to manifest anything in our lives, we need to feel. Emotions with thoughts create reality. That is how things are manifested.

Everything we do on the day of the south in your vision quest relates to nurturing the child within us. That is the beginning of the healing: nurturing. Without proper nurturing, a child cannot grow fully and will not be healthy in body, mind, or spirit.

The love we feel for others can become distorted if the child within us did not feel loved as a child. Even the way we nurture ourselves can be distorted if the child within us was not truly nurtured in childhood. The adult self takes direction by what has happened in one's childhood.

There are many ways to heal childhood traumas. On the shamanic path, we do not see life as past, present, or future. Life does not happen in a linear way; for us, life happens in a circular way. Our ancestors saw that and passed on that knowledge; therefore, it is very much possible to reach to the south of our medicine shield and heal the child, change our childhood memories and energy into a more positive and nurturing childhood, and bring more love to the child within.

However, as it is with every spiritual path, work is always required. One needs to look deep within in order to heal oneself. There is no pretending or skipping; one has to fully immerse oneself in one's wounds, touch them, clear them, and shift them, in order to truly heal. Without healing the wounded child, the adult self is unable to move forward fully, love fully, or connect fully.

The child within is so important in one's adult life that it forms the base of everything; it is the foundation that holds the house strong and solid.

So when you sit in our vision quest and you have a full day dedicated to your childhood, it is an opportunity to learn all the ways your inner child likes living life and all the things that make your child self happy.

In my childhood, I did not have proper nurturing. My family was very poor. My father could never hold a job, so my mother, who struggled with her mental health and suffered from bipolar disorder all her life, was the anchor and provider for our family. She performed miracles bringing us up, taking into consideration the fact that every two years her manic episodes sent her to hospital for three to six months at a time, which was always a time of uncertainty for us children. Then Mother would come home depressed, having the lows. There was sometimes no food on the table during those times, so when we were very young, often we were sent away to be looked after by others. Up to the age of nine, we were sent to be cared for by aunties or grandmothers, or sometimes sent to friends. From a very early age, as young as six years old, I had to learn to cook and tidy up for the family and grow responsible. So my childhood was cut short.

Often when one's south shield needs healing, one operates in the shadow of that shield. In my case, resentment in adulthood was one of my shadows coming from my wounded south shield. I resented always having to be the one who took care of everyone; I resented having to be the one to take the initiative for things and projects; I resented always having to be the one to make decisions; and so on. That resentment prevented me from coming into my full power as a leader for a long time. I could not be a good leader for my community because resentment would always creep in and hold me back. The difficulty is that when one is in the shadow self, which is unconscious, one does not know it. Deep work within the self is the only way to realise this and bring oneself out of the darkness. I am still working on my south shield; it seems a never-ending job.

To understand the child, we need to look with the heart of a child. Otherwise, we are just unbalanced adults causing more trauma to the inner child.

To spend a whole day in a vision quest in touch with the child within truly is a gift. We can look back and fully be ourselves. We can change things and memories and make things the way we want them to be. We are now empowered, supported by our loving guides and our loving ancestors, and therefore we are strong enough to do this kind of work with the self.

South medicine awakens the child's perception of the world. It brings the light of the sun to one's day. It brings new refreshing ideas into one's life. The child within has hopes and dreams, and without those hopes and dreams, one's life is useless, unsavoury, no fun! If we have an imbalanced south shield, all our life we will speak only of our troubles, forgetting to see all the good things we have around us.

One of the biggest emotions in the south is fear—fear of being seen, fear of being attacked by something bigger than us, fear of not being able to survive in a world where only the greatest, the biggest, and the most intelligent survive, and so on.

Fear begins in the solar plexus and spreads to the heart. It brings imbalance to the rational mind. We need to learn to close our solar plexus at the onslaught of fear. By having an awareness that fear wants to enter our system, we can slam the door in its face. We need to learn soul retrieval to bring back the parts of us that were lost in our childhood.

Where is your emotion at this moment in your life? Have you closed your emotions in order to cope? Have you closed your feelings in order to survive? If so, you need to find the tap that you closed and open it.

South medicine is also about love. When we reconnect ourselves with love, our south shield balances itself. The child in each one of us knows only to love. Holding and embodying the eternal flame of unconditional love and compassion gets us to a deeper level on our spiritual path. However, without healing our childhood traumas, holding and embodying unconditional love and compassion on our spiritual path is a long way away.

While you are on your quest and working with the south, you can also heal your relationship with water. Water is the element of the south. Do you drink enough water? Do you nourish the child in you with water? Do you nourish the cells in your body with water? Do you drink water with gratitude in your heart?

Lack of water in the body causes the cells in the body to struggle. It brings headache and does nothing to help the kidneys. It makes a person feel sluggish and tapped of energy.

Going to a deeper level: Do you help keep the water in the rivers and oceans clean? Do you treat water with respect? Everything is a mirror. What you do on this earth can cause you and others disease or other health issues.

It is important to balance your emotions, but it is equally important to balance your body and your spirit. Your spirit came here with a greater mission than mere survival or accumulation of material things. The way you relate to water in the grand scale of life is very important for your spiritual development and your relationship with humanity. Your positive relationship with water allows your spirit to flourish—and it is your spirit that connects you to humanity and all that is.

Your relationship with water informs the way you relate to all creatures on this earth. All beings on this earth are relations to one another. By seeing this, you heal the separation in yourself.

The people who live in the southern hemisphere are people well in touch with their emotions. They tend to live happy, joyful lives because they let their emotions flow. They tend to laugh more than the people who live in the northern hemisphere.

Your relationship with your body is also of paramount importance while you are working in the southerly direction. Have you healed yourself enough so that you have a good relationship with your body? Do you respect your body and give to it, or do you enslave your body and make it work constantly without rest? Do you abuse your body in any way?

You can balance the emotions and the anxieties that sit in the opposite direction—the north, the adult self—by navigating the axis of south and north of your inner wheel of life. Look into the north and bring the element of air into your lungs. Take time to breathe in and breathe out. Do it slowly, with awareness.

Like a child, connect with your body when you are working with the south medicine. Do some movement to help you to get in touch with your body. Do some yoga or tai chi or dance—any gentle movement to align your body, for if your body is well and balanced, it will make your vision quest much more comfortable. And in the grand scale of life, it will bring more comfort to your life too.

When working with the southerly direction in your vision quest, you can do a small ceremony to heal the child and bring it home by lighting a candle and singing your child self back home. You can let the sun from the south bless you and illuminate you. Let the warmth of the sun warm the heart of the child within you.

Day 2: The West

One wakes up on the second day looking into the west of one's circle of life. The west shield is the place of introspection and strength, and as such it is a fascinating place of the teenager self. The element in the west is earth, representing the human body. Again one benefits from positioning oneself physically looking into the west on that day.

The west shield, for some, can be difficult, while for others it can be the best direction to work with. It can represent, at some level, a death process in one's life. It also represents one's teenage years. Something ends in the west, and a day looking into the west might help you identify what it is that is dying in your personal life. Here you have the time to be fully with it, identify it, and let it go. The west brings one to introspection, to a place of looking deep within. There are always things or people in one's life that one hangs on to even though it is painful and difficult work. The west invites you to look at that. Why are you hanging on to people or ideas? Is it to do with keeping with what is familiar, with what you are comfortable with? There are different ways of holding on to something or someone and yet not grasping. You can do it without suffering or without carrying the weight on your shoulders.

The west invites you to look deep inside and learn from your experiences. It teaches you what is valuable to keep and what you truly need to let go of. Why do you keep banging your head against the wall? Why do you keep relationships with people who are not enhancing your life and just drag you down? Why do you allow that into your life? Why do you keep jobs that suck the light out of your soul, making your life meaningless? Why do you keep yourself stuck in darkness, depression, or suffering?

One needs to look deep inside oneself to find the answers. There is no one outside oneself who can give the answers. One is going to have to dig deep.

The west is also the place of rest. Rest. Peace. Quiet. There is nowhere to go, and there is nothing to do but to go within.

Here in the west there is an opportunity to look at your relationship with your body. Movement, yoga, tai chi, dance, making love—all that and more—allows you to be in your body. We all came to this earth to experience life in a body, so a good healthy relationship with the body is very important.

Do you respect your body the way it should be respected? Do you look after it, nurture it well, and listen to it? Putting healthy foods into your body and treating your body well is how you will keep it healthy to the end.

The relationship you keep with people tells how healthy your energy system is. Do you surround yourself with people who are uplifting, kind, and positive? Or do you surround yourself with people who are critical, judgemental, and negative? Relationships with people are choices you can make, in the same way that the foods you eat are choices.

The people you have around you can provide information on the kind of person you are. Are you a negative person? Do you put yourself down? The west is calling you to look deep indeed. Are you demanding? What kind of person are you? Are you harsh with yourself? Look around you, and look at the people around you, and you will know a bit more about yourself. The people who surround you are your mirror.

Looking into the west also has another objective: to find your inner gifts. What is it that you are good at? What is it that comes naturally and easily to you that you can share with others? What is it that your soul is passionate about? Those are the treasures you hold within yourself. It is now time to name them and bring them out into the world.

In your wounds, you find your gifts and your treasures. Look farther beyond adolescence; look deep into childhood and all of your life. What is it that made you stronger? What is it that made you who you are today? There, right there in your wounds, you will find your gifts. Right there is your treasure. Right there in your wounds you will find your pure essence and who you truly are.

Here you are invited to go deeper because you need to look farther beyond your wounds. Go deep, much deeper: Have your wounds made you a compassionate person? Have your wounds made you angry? Then those are the gifts you have for sharing. Angry people are passionate people and are action-ready people. Compassionate people change the world.

The element in the west is earth. Here is an opportunity for you to look at your relationship with the earth. Earth is grounding, is peaceful, and is holding. How much do you work to heal the earth? Do you collect rubbish from the earth, or do you throw rubbish on the earth? Do you care if the earth is polluted and if pesticides are spilled into the earth? Do you eat organically and make sure the suppliers of your food do not use pesticides? Do you support organic growth in your area?

The west also invites you to look beyond the self. How much do you work towards healing humankind's relationship with the planet? Do you help with the healing of that relationship? What kind of contribution do you make in that respect? It does not need to be something big; a small contribution towards it is enough. If each one of us would do a small thing, then we would all end up with a beautiful collective and a balanced relationship with our Earth Mother.

Let us not forget our children and the future generations. We are the model they base themselves on. A small action will create a ripple that will reach many. The love that we pour into our actions, the authenticity of it, is what counts more than anything else.

The west also invites you to heal your relationship with those who have wounded you. Forgive and release it so you can walk in the light.

In the wheel of life, you will encounter people who hurt you. It is as if they test your strength by pushing you around and wounding you. When that happens, you need to be strong. You are called to find your strength within, who you truly are. It is important not to let yourself be swept into self-pity, victimhood, or darkness when your ego is wounded.

Your connection to the earth can tell you who you are and show you your strength. Connecting to the earth gives you deep roots. Deep roots prevent you from being swept away easily by other people's ideas, judgements, or actions.

We are children born from the earth, who is our mother. She gives us our life, feeds us, nurtures us, and nourishes us. Therefore, our relationship with her is of paramount importance.

The west invites you to look into your shadow self, the "ugly" side that you and no one else wants to see. It is a deep initiation to welcome the shadow and realise its potential. Are you going to live in the shadow, or are you going to bring yourself into the light?

Your fears, your judgements, your shortcomings, the "serial killer" within you, are all invited to come into your awareness to heal. You can do this either consciously or subconsciously. In working with the west of your medicine shield, all that you are is invited to come forward for understanding and healing.

The shadow and the ego are very much part of being human. You must not push them away; on the contrary, you must call them forth. To be whole, you need to seek to understand all aspects of yourself.

When you find yourself bored or depressed, it is because you are passing through the west of your personal inner wheel. It is important to honour the feelings you have at this time. If the feeling is to let go and do something else or try something else in your life, then you must listen and do that, otherwise boredom and depression will stay for a very long time. The west is a time for gentleness with the self, to listen to the voice within. It is not a time for too much doing; it is a time to sit in silence and contemplation and truly listen within.

The west shield is the place of our dreams and visions, the place where we form a friendship with that side of ourselves that dreams of big things and projects, new worlds, and new ways. The west will nurture these things quietly and will help whatever we're seeking to do create roots inside our being.

The west helps us to cross the boundaries of limitation, to think outside the box and explore territories we would not otherwise dream of exploring. There is a great sense of growth that lies deep within, waiting to be touched, explored, and expressed in the west.

When you find yourself in the west, it is a good time to explore thoughts that lead you to new ideas. Every new thing one creates begins with a thought. Therefore, when you find yourself in the west, you can allow your thoughts to create your dreams, which can be manifest when you are balanced in all your shields: east, south, west, and north. By consciously exploring and bringing balance to all your shields, by working with those directions in your life, you are enabled to be in your own centre, the centre of manifestation and balance.

The west is also an invitation to connect deep with one's roots and the roots of the plants. The roots of the trees grow deep into the earth, as do our own ancestral roots. When we find our own roots, we feel more at peace and more connected to the earth. A sense of belonging begins to emerge.

Many of our bodily illnesses come from our imbalance in the west. Inability to take time to rest brings a lot of stress, and stress causes most of the health problems we have. Inability to listen to our body is another cause. As the body gives us signals all the time, listening to it is wise and is very important for our general well-being.

In a vision quest, you will find that the longest day is the day you are working with the west energies. So you need to make sure you take time to rest, have a snooze. All that is part of the west, and it means you are fully tuned in.

For you to get through the west of your life, you need to look at the medicine available to you in the opposite direction: the east. The sun energy and the fire energy uplift the spirit and allow us to cope with the hard times that life throws at us.

Sitting or lying in the sun on the day when you are working with the west is a lovely thing to do. If the sun is nowhere to be seen, then you can make a fire and connect with the fire energy. Connecting with the opposite medicine along the axis of your medicine shield always helps you to feel more balanced.

The spirit of the vision quest, although it encompasses all directions, resides in the west because it takes us into deep questioning.

When the sun goes down in the west, everything is dark and gloomy. Everything changes. That is why passing through the west brings changes to one's life, in the same way that vision quest brings deep changes to one's life. Opportunities arise in the west to enjoy a rest and just be without the business of doing.

It is through the west that one can connect with our spirits in the easterly direction. This axis works like an invisible bridge: the spiritual bridge to us or to ourselves.

The day you are working with the west shield is a good day for meditation, because meditation helps you to sit in stillness, quieten the mind, and connect with the spirit within.

Massaging the body is also good when you are in the west. People suffering from depression benefit from touch and bodywork, which helps release the deep pain they have inside themselves. You can massage your legs, arms, and feet with the conscious intention to release from your body the pain, sadness, and sorrow from anything or anyone who caused it.

West medicine is deep and pure. Approached with deep awareness, it will fully enrich your life and the lives of those around you.

When in the west, it is a good time to take stock of your relationship to the rest of the world. Do you hide from the world? Or do you allow the world to see you? Are you usually open and friendly? Do you make friends with your neighbours, or do you pass by and never get to know who your neighbours are?

Do you want to go within all the time? Or do you allow yourself to be out there engaging with people and the world? Are you afraid to be seen? All these questions are pertinent to the westerly direction.

Boredom in the west is very common; it is a sign of one's inability to sit with one's own self. We are always keeping ourselves busy and are constantly entertaining others or being entertained by others. However, when we try to sit for a long time without distractions, we find it hard to do so, because we are never able to sit in stillness.

Here you will benefit from looking at your teenage years and determining what worked and what did not work. What traumas did you inflict upon yourself and others, and what traumas did others inflict on you?

Working with the westerly direction is an opportunity to look back and find patterns and behaviours. You might find that a lot of these started in your teenage years. One's teenage years are a time that informs a lot of who one is going to be in adulthood—the adventurer, the risk taker, or the one who puts up with a lot of shit, and so on. All of that begins to take shape during one's teenage years. Therefore, here is an opportunity to review your life and perhaps mend what needs to be mended, making it the way you really want it to be. Working with the west gives you an opportunity to dream your life consciously.

Going through the west can be hard sometimes. Outside the vision quest, we are able to recognise when we are in the west in our lives when we are going through a time of wanting to be away from everyone and everything, a time when we just want to sleep and have very little energy to give, a time when we are depressed and cannot see the light at the end of the tunnel. When we recognise these things in ourselves, it means we are in the west. I recommend yoga, tai chi, dance, and movement—any form of body movement—for such times. Connecting with the East direction: fire and all kinds of creativity also helps. However, sometimes just going fully into one's dark cave, curling up, and staying there is the best medicine one can give oneself.

The nights in a vision quest can be filled with significant dreams too, especially when one is working with the west. Dreams pertinent to the past are a sign that a soul retrieval is needed to correct a soul fragmentation which happened in the past. Spontaneous soul retrievals can happen in a vision quest as well—and all dreams are very important. One needs to be really paying attention to connect with the dreams, learn from them, and heal; they are pointers to what healing one needs next in one's life or what part of oneself is missing.

Once I dreamt of my first love while I was working with the west shield in a vision quest. I was about twelve or thirteen years old, and he was a cousin of mine. Nothing ever happened between us, but I felt I left a part of my soul with him; the dream told me that very clearly. In the dream, I could see how happy I was with his arrival; my heart was filled with love and with a sense of youthfulness and purpose again. More than forty years had passed, and I was never aware that I had experienced a soul loss in relation to the first time I fell in love. This soul loss had caused me to have constant dreams most of my adult life that I was always falling in love with someone, when in reality, it was my lost soul part that was falling in love for the first time. Repeated dreams are very powerful clues of soul loss. It was only after this dream in the vision quest that I could understand the recurring dream and the origin of the problem and then heal myself.

Once in another vision quest I had a dream about my time as a teenager playing volleyball for my school team. We used to travel to other cities to play against other schools. I was young and strong, happy to be part of something which I considered big. It was a time when I really built up my self-esteem. When I was a child living in poverty and with a mother who was bipolar, every little bit of self-worth I'd had was bitten out of me. Looking back, I see that being part of that team and having been selected for it because I was good at volleyball really helped me and made a huge impact in my life. I now understand why I put so much energy into my projects and make them work, especially when to do so seems totally against the odds. No matter what, I never give up. Our wounds make us who we are.

Soul loss does not occur because of trauma alone; soul lost can also occur when parts of a person stay where they are because they are really happy there.

So, how can you bring a soul part home once you become aware you have lost it? You can sing, calling your soul back to your heart, or you can talk and negotiate with it. You can light a candle and illuminate the path so that soul part can find it's way back home. Sometimes you need to convince your soul part that it is much better to be there with you as both you and the soul part will be stronger together. Sometimes you have to promise something to the soul part. However, you must be very careful with what you promise as it needs to be something you can deliver. Otherwise, the soul part will go back to the place where it was before if that place is a much happier place.

On the other hand, if the soul loss occurred because you have had a trauma, it is much easier to bring it back once you become aware of the loss. When such is the case, no negotiations are required. Mostly, the soul will desperately want to come home to the self but does not know how to do so or does not know if it is safe yet. Becoming aware of it, calling it, and guiding it back will illuminate the path back home to your heart.

If soul loss occurred because you have cast a part of your soul away, then some tough negotiations will be required to bring it back. Sometimes, we send a part of ourselves away because we, or others, cannot cope with it or deal with it. Perhaps we are ashamed of it. For those parts of yourself that you have sent away, you will need negotiation skills to convince them to return. If you promise anything to a soul part, you must do it, or you run the risk of losing it again.

Soul loss can leave a person completely disempowered. Often it is one's trust, love, compassion, confidence, memory, or health that goes with it. Bringing the soul part home can only bring big changes. The energy of that work, however, is very subtle. One needs to be tuned in with the self in order to notice the subtle yet powerful change. Soul retrieval is one of the simplest yet most powerful ways of healing the self. What is healing? Healing is simply what happens when a shift in consciousness, a shift in the way one feels, thinks, or is, occurs and changes things for the better.

In my last vision quest, I really struggled in the west. The spirits were waking me up every hour, clearly wanting me to do some work. I was very tired, exhausted physically, mentally, and emotionally. I had used all the energy I had in the middle of the night to sit up. I cried a deep cry and began to tell the spirits how tired I was. I needed more help to cope with the workload I had on my hands. I was working too much and holding many charitable projects. Not only that, but also the cases I was getting for shamanic healing were becoming more and more difficult. I was undoing black magic, undoing curses, retrieving people's powers that had been taken by a sorcerer, removing poisonous energetic arrows from people, and dealing with clients' mental health problems. The list could go on. I was also starting to go through the menopause, so things were pretty hard for me. On top of that, I was really struggling physically as my body was no longer the same. My yoga practice was helping, but when I would miss a day of yoga because I was too busy, my stress level would get really high. Yes, I needed some vitamin supplements to help me, but equally, I needed more spirits to help me with the spiritual work, plus more people to help me in the physical world. Something had to happen: I had to move from doing to being, but I did not know how.

I sat there sobbing like a little child unable to cope, and then I cried myself to sleep as I used to do when a child.

You have to truly enter darkness in the west; something in you has to die, and a ceremony has to be performed. So, on the night of the west, when it is really dark, you should perform a death lodge ceremony. Collect a few stones to represent the people who support you in your life. In my case, I prefer to always bring out my personal inner council. They are the guides who help me and support me.

How many people you have there is not important. What is important is that you truly feel loved and supported by those you choose to be with you for your death lodge ceremony.

My personal inner council is composed of several guides: the chief, the elder, the warrior, the healer, the Goddess, the inner child, the ancestors, and my animal spirit helper.

Each supporter will have a stone to represent him or her in your ceremony. Call the people or the spirits one by one as you put each stone in a circle around you to represent them. Do this in a ceremonial way. Everything in a vision quest is a ceremony. Then call all the people one by one from your life whom you have unfinished business with, all the people who have caused you trauma or pain, or all the people who bother you in one way or another. Equally, call the people whom you cause or have caused trauma or pain. This is a great opportunity to resolve all your unfinished business.

The death lodge ceremony is done when it is pitch-dark, for there is power in the darkness. One by one, call to the edge of your sacred lodge each person you have unfinished business with. Have a heart-to-heart talk, a moment of truth. Express your feelings and give the person the opportunity to express his or her feelings. Perform this lodge ceremony as if it is your last day on this earth and this is your opportunity to make things right. This ceremony is a good way to bring healing on all levels. After a person has had his or her say, release the person and either send him or her away or invite him or her to stay in your sacred circle. Carry on until all the people have been called and all the work is done. Only after that should you go back to your sleeping place. Your west shield is then filled with power, but only when true healing is done.

Day 3: The North

The third day of the quest is dedicated to the north of our circle of life. The element here is air, representing the mind, which is in constant flow.

Often it is common to have a visit from the winds on the third day of one's quest. They come to honour the quester and to be honoured.

The north is the place of clarity, the place of wisdom, and as such, it is also the place of our ancestors. In the north, we celebrate our mind and adulthood; here we also celebrate community.

It is because of the creative mind that we keep ourselves busy, trying to fulfil this and that in our lives, investing our energy in new projects, and so on. The mind is the masterpiece of Creation, but you must always make sure yours is balanced. If it is out of balance, your mind can create drama. So, ask yourself, "What is it that my mind is creating? Is it creating good things, or it is creating fears, anxieties, judgements, dramas?" You must always check within and make sure you are one step ahead of your mind. To be balanced, you need to have your heart, mind, and spirit aligned. Otherwise, sometimes the mind goes loopy, which makes things very hard. Also, your mind is supposed to be your helper and not your boss. More often than not, the mind wants to be the boss and does not give the heart an opportunity to be. You have to tame your mind so it serves you and not the other way around.

Practising mindfulness and meditation helps, as does practising becoming aware of each thought you have every second of your day, which is extremely important. I am not good at sitting and meditating, but I am good at being aware of each thought I have and changing my thoughts when needed.

What we think is what we create, so we need to be aware twenty-four hours a day of what it is that we are manifesting with our thoughts.

There is nothing akin to the mind—no power is equal to the powers of the mind—and therefore it is important that we learn to tame the mind and make it work for us. When we manage to do that, we begin to attain spiritual powers.

A quality that one finds in the northerly direction is service, service to people, service to the community, service to one's family. When you sit looking into the north, you can ask Spirit if you have been called to serve in a different way from the way you have been serving. It is good to ask if the way you are serving truly is service or if you are being called to serve in a different way.

There are numerous ways to serve. One can serve on a small scale or a grand scale. Neither is more or less important than the other; they are just different ways of serving. So you need to look deep within your heart to find the answer to how you can serve.

A vision quest can help you identify the changes you need to make. It will take a year for that information to fully integrate into your energy, your psyche, and your body.

The vision quest is about change, change from one thing to another or from one way to another. It is important to identify and recognise what it is that blocks you from reaching your full potential. Once you identify it with a very deep enquiry, by which I mean a very serious enquiry, then you can work slowly through those blockages and hammer them one by one. This work may take months and sometimes years.

I have concluded that a vision quest is not for the faint-hearted. First of all, the hardship it presents already puts a lot of people off. Ayahuasca is the same; the fear and the hardship that surrounds these two medicines is a testimony of the power they hold. We could hide behind fears, but then what is fear really serving?

It is important to know oneself well when one is walking a spiritual path. It is important to know one's weaknesses and strengths. In walking a spiritual path, one needs to expand. There is little point in staying in the same place forever. Equally, that expansion needs to be sought and carefully integrated into one's energy field and day-to-day life. Otherwise, one runs the risk of burning out. One needs to be practical and organise things in one's lives in a practical way and with the guidance of Spirit.

We co-create with Spirit, yet we are human beings limited by the physical body. It is important to honour one's body, mind, and spirit in the process of co-creating with Spirit.

No rush; there is no need to rush anything. All that is needed is to be in the here and now, yet always seeking to expand the mind, the heart, and the spirit.

The northerly direction is also the place of the ancestors. The ancestors bring clarity and wisdom to the mind and the heart. Connecting with our ancestors makes us stronger people. Knowing our history, where we come from, empowers us and the generations to come.

In the ancestral line, we will find gifts, but we will also find traumas passed down from one generation to another. These traumas need healing. We can do healing work with seven generations before ourselves, and twelve generations will be able to hear us if our cry is deep and sincere. The ancestors are bound to us in the same way we are bound to them. That means when we call, they come. It is important to connect with the ancestors in the spiritual realm. When we acknowledge them, they acknowledge us.

Ancestors do not stay around us all the time, but just like guides, they are one thought away from us; calling them from the heart is enough for them to come. The reason why they do not stay around us all the time is that after they disincarnate, they still have work to do on the other side, so they continue growing and expanding spiritually, just the same. Calling them in times of need is good. Praying for them is also good. Our prayers reach their hearts and help them with their work too. Sometimes, just like us, they also need help.

Claiming our ancestral line and healing is a huge responsibility in itself. We cannot connect to the land without connecting to our ancestors. We cannot connect to the trees without connecting to the ancestors. The spirits of the ancestors are everywhere and in everything.

When we are working with the north shield, singing a song for the ancestors is very empowering. The trees told me that when we sing for our ancestors, twelve generations before will hear our song.

In talking about the ancestors, we have to talk about future generations too. One day we will become the ancestors. Sending prayers for our descendants will strengthen them; our prayers will reach them in times of need. In the same way, we can work with seven generations before us and also work with seven generations ahead of us; they can all be called, healed, and strengthened just like anyone who exists in the present.

Celebrating the ancestors and future generations is a lovely thing to do. Gathering flowers and offering them to past generations and future generations brings joy to our hearts and theirs; it strengthens our bloodline and reinforces our bond.

The northerly direction is the realm of the mind, intellect, knowledge, and wisdom. If we look at the northern hemisphere of our planet, we see that most of the northern people are very much mind orientated. Degrees and education are very important for the northern people of our planet. There is nothing wrong with that, because knowledge and intellect create a happy heart. The only problem is when the priority of nurturing the mind prevails over the priority of nurturing the heart.

Great inventions have been created in the northern hemisphere because the gifts of the mind are highly developed in the north.

Often there will be one direction that you will find hardest to work with. That direction is the one you have the most to learn from. It will help you heal, embrace, and let go. For me, the hardest direction in my first vision quest was the southerly direction because I had to heal traumas from my childhood. Then in my second vision quest, it was the westerly direction, and in my third vision quest, it was the northerly direction because I had to let go and heal my north shield, my adult self.

In my last vision quest, in working with the north, my healing was about embracing leadership and letting go of trying to figure everything out with my head. I was also working on healing my relationship with my ancestors. Although I have done a great deal of healing with my ancestral line in my life, I still have so much work to do.

Mental health problems are one of the things that were passed down my ancestral line. I have realised that my healing began in my teens, when I started to walk my spiritual path and also started to practise yoga. Walking the shamanic path and having a yoga practice balances my mind; it also balances my body and spirit. Because of this, I have always been healthy, mentally, physically, and emotionally; it is very rare for a disease to find a way into my system.

I have a mother, a grandmother, and a great-grandmother who suffered from poor mental health, and I was not prepared to be the next one in line. Manic depression, also called bipolar disorder, is a sad mental health condition indeed. To balance it, a lot of thought and hard work, and a holistic approach, is required. I have found that my spiritual shamanic path, together with yoga practice, truly balances me.

Feeling held by the spirits allows me to surrender and let go, especially at times when things seem to be completely, totally, and utterly falling apart and my life has become out of control, not to mention the lows I experience.

I have learnt to heal myself with ceremonies. Ceremonies are powerful, especially ceremonies that take us to the extreme and symbolise some sort of death, such as ayahuasca, vision quest, sweat lodge, and earth lodge; these are four medicines very dear to my heart. When I notice I am not able to cope, before I go into full crisis mode, I perform one of the foregoing ceremonies to die and be reborn. I do it consciously because I know that if I do not, my soul will do it for me and life will be unbearable for quite some time. Life keeps bringing in initiations all the time, so we might as well choose to consciously create and go through those initiations ourselves and be empowered.

Ceremonies help me to cope and to put into perspective whatever is going on in my life. When I cannot cope with life any more, I look for the medicine that will help me. Sometimes I put myself inside an earth lodge and stay there for two or three days fasting in the darkness, talking to the spirits and healing. I always come back completely renewed, with a new sense of purpose and clarity.

A sense of profound balance follows big ceremonies. Ceremonies as medicine should be in our everyday life really, as a way to balance the chaos and harshness of life. Ceremonies help us to make sense of things, especially when life is making no sense. They help us to focus, recalibrate, and rebalance. It is as if we must acknowledge the unseen in order to cease creating chaos in our lives.

Here in the north of the self, in the north of our vision quest, it is good to ask the spirit of vision quest what is required of us in order to go through our third day of fasting and isolation.

Isolation is not a problem for me, but fasting is. As a person with low blood sugar levels, fasting really throws me out. Whereas some people become energised and feel fully alive, I get very weak and can hardly move by the third day. So, here is an opportunity to ask the spirits of the north, the ancestors, what it is that is required from us; what are the next steps in our lives, and how can we take those steps? When we are weak, when we can no longer take a step forward, then this is a good opportunity to ask the help of the ancestors for taking our next step. Often we know what that step is, but our resistance is so huge that we really make things harder for ourselves without needing to do so. Our soul, our spirit, want to take that big step, but our minds fight it. In the north, we benefit from doing a little ceremony for the mind, lighting a candle, saying a prayer, or doing a dance—if our physical body allows it.

Often at this point in the third day of fasting, the mind begins to lose grip of itself. We become disorientated; we cannot think straight and cannot make sense of anything. However, this is a good thing, because we have arrived exactly where we need to be, a place where we are open, where the spirits can talk to us without our dismissing them. I would say that there needs to be a crack so the spirits can come in.

Our minds will do everything to convince us to give up. We need to be astute enough to recognise when our mind is doing this. This is not to say that the mind is not necessary; on the contrary, the mind is really important. But on the spiritual path, the mind is not the boss; the spirit is. If the mind was allowed to be the boss, we would most certainly not walk a spiritual path, as the mind does not understand such a path. The mind cannot make sense of a spiritual path; therefore, it does not support a path that is spiritual.

That is why the alignment of mind, heart, and spirit is so important. With the alignment, each part of a person, the mind, heart, and spirit, knows the person's worth and his or her work. Each part respects one the others and gives way to them. Peace reigns within when things are like that. Decisions that the heart makes, the mind accepts; decisions that the spirit makes, the heart and the mind support without conflict or hardship. Decisions that the heart and the spirit cannot make, they ask the mind. When things are like this, one is balanced and wise and is using all one's faculties in perfect balance and harmony.

It is the spirit that makes decisions on a vision quest, not the mind. Gentle energy at all levels is required to deal with certain matters and decisions coming from the spirit. Once we come to a place of vulnerability, something in us opens. That is when most of the healing work takes place. We then have that single moment of realisation and illumination, which can happen at any point in our vision quest. We just need to be paying attention and we will see that moment arise.

The north also represents the community. The way we relate to the community is very important. The community represents our sense of well-being and generosity of spirit. For us to live in the community, we need generosity of spirit. Living with other people requires that. Everyone has some level of generosity of spirit. So what is a generosity of spirit? It is giving truly from the heart without expecting anything in return. Indigenous people are born with a generosity of spirit. They share everything: what is mine is yours.

The community also teaches us to be selfless. The smallest community in existence is the family unit, where everyone lives together and shares many things. The wisdom of living in a community means waste can be avoided—waste of energy, waste of material things, etc. The earth benefits from people living in a community. So do the people.

When we fully become adults, we have a good balance of service within ourselves, which means a good relationship with the community can unfold. Love and compassion are required to complete the north shield. We are not made to live alone; the human spirit rejoices when we get together with others who share the same interests as we have. Great projects are created when a community comes together. And when that happens, the collective benefits, not just one person.

Looking into the north, into one's adult self, brings a sense of balance, understanding, and purpose to one's life. When Sara Beauregard and I co-founded Youth Vision Scotland in 2006, our intention was to provide young people with a meaningful and safe way to make the transition from childhood to adulthood. Providing rites of passage for young people is a way of creating a healthy community of young spirited souls whose souls are too big to fit into the box of a classroom. Youth Vision participants are young people who are struggling with life in general. Often, our young people need to be held for a little while longer while they are completing their transition to the adult world. Youth Vision offers a safe space for that to happen and helps the young people during their transformation. A little bit like a butterfly inside a cocoon, Youth Vision is the cocoon that holds and protects the young people as their lives unfold.

The Planetary Healing Centre is another community I am part of, a group of beautiful like-minded people who uphold unconditional love and compassion for others. A team of volunteers work there, and they expect no payment or financial gain. Some have been there for seventeen years, others for fifteen years, others for ten years, others for five years, and so on. Some are young, some are adults, and some are grandmothers and great-grandmothers.

Spirit has told me that giving without expecting anything in return is the utmost spiritual attainment on a spiritual path. The reason why our

Planetary Healing Centre's community has managed to survive for so many years is because of the spirit of community and the spirit of giving. The spiritual attainment that we volunteers gain is the greatest gift we receive for our work.

In the north, the body will need to rest and the mind will need to relax so one can complete one's passage into the east, the place of Spirit. When working on the easterly direction, one will need to be awake for one's last night; therefore, it is important to take plenty of rest during the day while you are working with the north.

At the end, when you come out of the vision quest from the easterly direction, that is your new beginning.

Day 4: The East

Despite the difficulties, the feelings of giving up, the death process, the pain, and the discomfort, the sun will always rise, and so will the human spirit. And with that, the east comes. A new beginning is always on the cards and follows south, west, and north. New beginnings in one's life always arrive like the sun: gentle yet powerful, every day at the same time, without fail.

On the last day, one is filled with a sense of clarity and joy. Illumination of the east brightens one's day, and a new phase of life begins. One has gone through the trials, did not eat, did not sleep properly for four days and four nights. One has seen all one needed to see. One has cried all one's tears, has prayed, has given up, and has died a few deaths. In the death process, one found a few answers and a new sense of purpose. The quester has released what no longer serves him or her and has shed the last tear he or she could possibly shed.

The sunrise reminds us that, like the sun, we can rise again. Like the sun, we can bring brightness and joy to many who cross our path. Like the sun, our power is gentle yet strong.

A new day begins, and with a new day, a new life begins (east), one that is more based in love (south), more authentic (west), and clear (north). We have gone through the cycle of our lives and have healed some of our wounds; we have looked deep inside despite the fear, without interruption. We have balanced all that we are. We have connected to our ancestors, and our roots now grow strong. We have forgiven those who have harmed us, or we have cast such people away once and for all. We have prayed for those who are suffering. We have connected to the earth, who has held us safe and nurtured us in her arms. She has reminded us that we are not separated, that we are loved and are important, and that we are her children and she is our Mother.

A new sense of purpose awakens in us when we arrive in the east on our last day. A subtle yet very powerful sense of purpose arises, a purpose that was not there before. And we cannot wait for it to unfold in our day-to-day lives.

We see the sunrise, and with it comes a new form of illumination, new colours, and new vibrations. We feel renewed and ready to begin again.

Our senses are enhanced; we hear everything, every single bird, every drop of water. Now there seems to be more space in our hearts and minds, space for new connections, new ideas, and new love. And inside we find a strength we never had before.

A deep feeling of fulfilment fills us up. We greet the east as we might greet our best friend, with great joy, reverence, and respect. We feel joy in our hearts for the worst has passed and a new day, a new sunrise, completely fills us with joy and purpose again. That is how it should be and how we should live every day of our lives: filled with purpose.

As the Navajos say: *We need to recover our indigenous mind.* We all come from indigenous ancestors. How far back is not important. What is important is to recover our indigenous minds and memories. Our Earth Mother is calling for all her children to reunite, care for one another, and care for her.

We can revert pollution, we can revert greed, and we can educate ourselves and our children to live closer to the earth, to respect her and care for her. The earth is our only home. It is our duty to care for her and leave her intact for our children and grandchildren. A lot of healing is needed if we are going to be able to do that and begin to live a more balanced life.

So with the sun rising, we pack our things. We are now filled with a huge sense of purpose. In going through the ordeal of the vision quest, we have begun to remember who we are and to see the gentle strength that lies within.

As we leave our quest, we are ready to enter the centre of ourselves, the centre of balance. We are ready to live a more balanced life because we each remember how to be a child again, a happy child. We remember how to be a teenager and all the good things that come with that. We now remember how to be a balanced adult and how to be amidst community again. By remembering who we are and that the earth is our Mother, we remember that others are our brothers and sisters. Their struggle is our struggle; their suffering is our suffering; their Mother is our Mother. We remember that the animals, the insects, the birds, and all creatures share this earth with us and that the earth is their Mother too. All creatures, big and small, are our family. A new sense of joy begins to emerge as we feel connected. We are ready to return home to our family, to our friends, and to life, but we are coming home stronger, different, and truly empowered.

To have balance, we need to be in the centre of our circle of life looking into the south, coming from the hearth. At the same time, we need to be able to turn and look into the west and introspect. We need to be able to look into the north, have clarity, and make great decisions in our life. In the same way, we need to be able to look into the east and begin again when life requires us to begin again. To be in the centre and able to reach out to all aspects of ourselves and be in balance is to be in a place of empowerment.

So it is that we stand up. As we do so, we have a circle of energy, a circle of power, around us. We have worked hard for four days and nights to acquire this power. That circle of power protects us and supports us.

Afterword

So, this is my story, the story of a woman who slowly began to remember who she is. I began to reconnect with my roots, and through that process, I found who I truly am and realised that I come from the earth and that to her I will one day return.

Shamanism as Medicine has given me the opportunity to heal, the opportunity to empower myself and walk taller and stronger.

It is my hope that *Shamanism as Medicine* brings joy to your heart and helps you, too, to remember who you are, which will help you heal yourself, empower yourself, and heal and empower others along the path.

About the Author

Cláudia Gonçalves was born in Minas Gerais, in the southeast of Brazil and she holds a deep honour for the Sacred Healing tradition passed down to her from her indigenous grandmothers.

Cláudia started to develop spiritually at the age of 13 years old guided by elder Dona Mercedes. This was the start of her spiritual shamanic path which she takes very seriously and with full time dedication.

She moved to the UK in 1994, embarking on a profound journey of personal transformation. In 2001 her indigenous great-grandmother's spirit came to her in a sweat lodge ceremony, summoning her to go back to her roots and start doing shamanic work. Seclusion, deep inner work receiving teachings directly from the Spirits and training with outside teachers began; a year later, 2002, she started to work as a full time shamanic practitioner serving the community in the UK.

Co-founder of The Edinburgh Shamanic Centre, The Community Foundation for Planetary Healing and the Youth Vision Scotland, Cláudia works with people in Scotland and people all over the world; a great part of her work is also dedicated to various Indigenous groups in Brazil.

You can also see a glimpse of Cláudia's work in the documentary "The Edge of Dreaming" by Scottish film director Amy Hardy - 2009.

www.shamaniccentre.com | www.planetary-healing.org | www.youthvision.uk | www.holistic-shop.co.uk | www.claudiagoncalves.com